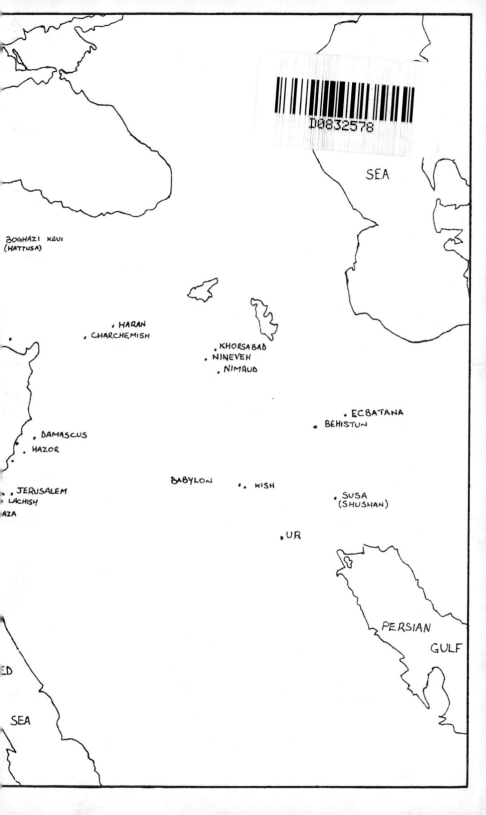

SEA

BOGHAZI KEUI
(HATTUSA)

. HARAN
. CHARCHEMISH

. KHORSABAD
. NINEVEH
. NIMAUD

. ECBATANA
. BEHISTUN

. DAMASCUS

. HAZOR

BABYLON   . . KISH

. JERUSALEM
LACHISH

AZA

. SUSA
(SHUSHAN)

. UR

PERSIAN

GULF

ED

SEA

DUAL HERITAGE

The Bible and The British Museum

Norman S Prescott

To the memory of
the Rev L T Pearson MA(Cantab) Hon CF
(1884-1978)
who first set my feet
on the Bible evidences road.

ISBN 0 904378 31 4

Cover: initial design by Joel M Prescott (Aged 10)

Published in 1986
by
Cortney Publications
Bainson House, Alton Road, Luton, Beds.

Produced by Inprint of Luton Ltd.
95-115 Windmill Road, Luton, Beds. LU1 3XS

CONTENTS

ILLUSTRATIONS

FOREWORD
by
Lt Col K W Sear, General Secretary Soldiers' and Airmen's Scripture Readers Association, and Miss Daniell's Soldiers' Homes

THE HAND OF GOD IN THE HISTORY OF MAN

This book has been written because what it says is too valuable to go unrecorded. Norman Prescott, the author, has a special interest in the British Museum and the fascinating testimony which many of its exhibits give to the historical accuracy of the Bible. I felt that the good things which God had shown him ought not to be wasted but shared with as many as possible. And from this came the vision of organising his material in book form so that others too might enjoy and profit from his discoveries.

It is not a "dry as dust" tome through which the reader will have to plod wearily, but is written in an engaging and lively style with spiritual truths and applications constantly emerging. One is left with a sense of awe and wonder as the hand of God is seen at work in the secular history of man and brought to life for us in "Dual Heritage — The Bible and The British Museum".

I was introduced to Norman Prescott by Andrew Purslow, the Army Scripture Reader at Aldershot whom God used to bring me to Christ. Since then his friendship and fellowship have meant a great deal to me. He is one of those delightful Christians who has always just discovered some new spiritual treasure from the Bible and as he shares this one feels not only informed but refreshed and uplifted. I am particularly indebted to him for his unbounded and infectious enthusiasm for the authority of scripture as being, and not just containing, the revealed Word of God. As you read his book I trust the same enthusiasm will lay hold of you and not only add to your knowledge but encourage you in your witness for the Lord.

The author's profits from the book will be given to the work of The Soldiers' and Airmen's Scripture Readers Association and the Miss Daniell's Soldiers' Homes for the furtherance of their evangelical work among the Forces. Both organisations are Bible based and seek to present the Word of God to young service men and women so that they might come to know for themselves the God of the Word.

INTRODUCTION

The suggestion was made to me by Lt Col K W Sear, General Secretary of the Soldiers' and Airmen's Scripture Readers Association (SASRA), that I assume the task of writing an up-to-date version of Mrs A R Habershon's book of 1909, *The Bible and the British Museum*.

This project has been undertaken over a period of several years, with the encouragement and help of staff at the Museum. The main object of the book (as was Mrs Habershon's) is to confirm and strengthen belief in the historical validity and accuracy of the Word of God as we have it in our English Bible.

In places where appropriate, Mrs Habershon's words have been used, but much is new as the Museum has greatly changed since her day and many new discoveries have been made in the archaeological and philological fields, such as the Isaiah scrolls of the Dead Sea.

"There are many whose faith in the veracity of the Scriptures has been shaken, and the best way to re-establish their faith is to show them that the charges which are brought against the Bible are untrue and unwarranted.

The Old Testament narratives are in harmony with all that is really known of the history of the world in the times described in the Old Testament records . . . the events recorded and the persons and things described are true to history. The Biblical narrative is derived from written sources based on contemporaneous documents. An extraordinary confirmation of the careful transmission of the Hebrew documents from original sources lies in the exact manner in which the names of the kings of Egypt, Assyria, Babylon, etc, are spelled. That the Hebrew writers should have transliterated these names with such accuracy and conformity to philological principles is a wonderful proof of their thorough care and scholarship and of their access to the original sources. That the names should have been transmitted through so many copyings and so many centuries in so complete a state of preservation is a phenomenon unequalled in the history of literature" (*Which Bible*, ed David Otis Fuller, DD).

In Mrs Habershon's day there was much public interest in the Bible and the British Museum; great crowds filled Fleet Street eagerly awaiting editions of the newspapers with reports of the latest archaeological discoveries, the results of which were being brought to the Museum. Today it is different. During a recent visit to the Museum an overseas visitor asked, "Where are the British people?" The answer is, "Mainly absent." Except for special events, the Museum is used largely by parties of school children, minority religious groups and visitors from overseas.

Much change has taken place in the Museum over recent years and is still going on, so that it is not possible to give an exact guide to the whereabouts of all the objects mentioned. In fact, some of Biblical interest may soon no longer be on display as the general emphasis moves from Biblical discovery to such subjects as the development of writing.

So, while many of the original Bible exhibits are still on view, let us make our way to the Museum.

My appreciation and thanks are due to staff in various departments of the Museum who so generously gave of their interest and time to the project — particularly to Dr Irving L Finkel of the Western Asiatic Antiquities Department for his warm interest and encouragement. Also to Glyn and Audrey Jenkins of Aylesbury for editing and typing the script, and to Norman J Gurney of Cortney Publications without whose help and interest this book could not have been produced.

It is with extreme gratitude that I record the provision of the friends who so willingly gave of their time and ability to do the final editing and correcting of the script.

As has already been mentioned, it was the initiative of Lt Col K W Sear that launched this project which he has so generously sponsored and encouraged, with the warm support of his wife Mrs Norma Sear. Ken Sear and I are at one in sending this book forth in the trust that it will be used in renewing, strengthening and confirming faith in the Bible.

Finally, this book is not intended primarily as a guide book but rather as a fireside tour of the Museum and its treasures which support the veracity of the Bible.

Norman S Prescott
86 West Street
Farnham, Surrey
GU9 7EN
January 1986

The British Museum: Main Entrance in Gt. Russell St., London, WC1

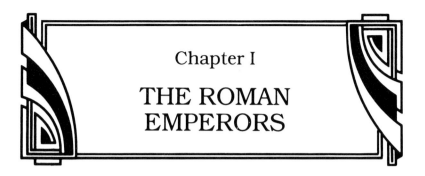

Chapter I

THE ROMAN EMPERORS

"Bible students in the British Museum have two special requirements. First they need help in finding the objects which are of most interest, and second they want to be able to look at the passages of Scripture illustrated by the monuments. In this volume, an endeavour is made to meet these two requirements" (*The Bible and the British Museum*, Ada R Habershon).

Since Mrs Habershon's book was published in 1909 the Museum has undergone great change. The displays are being modernised and made very attractive. Also new exhibits which were not available in her day are now to be seen there. It seems therefore worthwhile to attempt an up-to-date work for a new generation of Bible readers. This book is such an attempt, expanded perhaps somewhat beyond the confines of the original but deriving its inspiration and background from that excellent volume.

CYRENIUS

"And it came to pass in those days, that there went out a decree from **Caesar Augustus**, that all the world should be taxed. (And this taxing was first made when Cyrenius was Governor of Syria.)" (Luke 2 vv 1–2).

Over the years as archaeology and scholarship have revealed more and more facts of past history, so has the Bible record been authenticated, as Professor Sayce has pointed out in his book *Monument Facts and Higher Critical Fancies*. Professor Sayce was at one time a leading critic of the Bible but completely changed his ideas because of facts brought to light by archaeology.

1

Augustus

Tiberius

Nero

Vespasian

Titus   *Photographs: BM*

2

THE CENSUS

There has been much controversy over Luke's account of the census which brought Joseph and Mary to Bethlehem. Much of the difficulty only arises because of the tradition which places the birth of Jesus Christ as the year 1 AD. The late Rev L T Pearson used to say, "Tradition is always wrong." This may not be altogether so, but tradition without corroborative evidence to support it is a very shaky foundation on which to build.

In a report printed in the *Daily Telegraph* for 16th September 1985, Dr Percy Seymour, a Plymouth Polytechnic lecturer, is quoted as saying that the real date of Christmas was 15th September seven years before the traditional date of the Lord's birth.

Whilst not giving unqualified support to all of Dr Seymour's conclusions, there can be no doubt that he is on the right track, for the birth was undeniably at the time of the Feast of Tabernacles, September–October. Cornfeld's *Pictorial Biblical Encyclopedia*, a Jewish publication, gives Quirinius (the Cyrenius of Luke 2) as Legate of Syria from 11 to 8 BC. Another Hebrew source quotes Quirinius as 7 BC and the birth of Jesus as 6 BC, so that Dr Seymour is not alone in his dating. In Cornfeld there is a gap of one year before the rule of the next Governor of Syria. Either date will do, as the record says that the taxing was "first" made when Cyrenius was Governor of Syria. As a census of such magnitude would take a considerable period to prepare and accomplish, there need be no discrepancy and no question as to the accuracy of Luke's statement.

THE EMPERORS

In the British Museum are sculptural portraits of the Roman Emperors. In Mrs Habershon's day they were exhibited together in a line; at the time of writing (November 1985) they are exhibited on the upper floor in Room 70 on the Museum plan, as part of an exhibition called "The Image of Augustus". This is intended to be temporary, and at some future date a good deal of the material in it will be placed in a permanent exhibition illustrating Rome: The City and Empire.

Other examples of Roman sculpture, including some Emperors, may now be seen in the recently opened Wolfson Galleries in the basement, but the Emperors are in amongst many other examples of Greek and Roman portrait sculpture and have to be searched out. Let us then follow round the portraits as they are at present to be seen in the Augustus exhibition.

"But when the fulness of the time was come, God sent forth His Son, made of a woman, made under the law" (Galatians 4 v 4).

To get some understanding of the significance of this passage, let us first look at the portrait of **Julius Caesar**. Caesar, after a brilliant military career in Gaul, during which time he visited Britain, finally marched with his army to Rome to seize power. Having defeated Pompey he became, as one publication puts it, "the foremost man in all the world". He undertook the task of putting the affairs of the Roman Empire in order and making wise laws.

The time came when a group of conspirators plotted to slay him. They approached him on the pretext of presenting a petition and then drew their swords and stabbed him to death. Marcus Brutus, who had been treated with great favour by Caesar, was amongst the conspirators. It is said that when Caesar saw him with his sword drawn he uttered those famous words, "Et tu Brute." (And thou too, Brutus.)

The one destined to become the first Roman Emperor, his adopted son Octavian, was then only 18 years of age and no one thought that he could take the place of the great Caesar.

Marcus Antonius, a friend of the murdered Caesar, obtained leave to speak to the people and stirred up a great fury against the murderers. For a long time none knew which party would get the upper hand. The young Caesar (Octavian) made common cause with Antony and soon the parties were at war. Antony and Octavian overthrew the other party, of whom the most famous is Marcus Brutus, by reason of Shakespeare's play.

It seemed at first that Antony and Octavian would command the world; however, as both wished to rule, war broke out between them.

THE STAGE IS SET
"God moves in a mysterious way, His wonders to perform." It may appear a little strange to say, in the midst of such seeming chaos, that thus was the stage set for the "fulness of

the time" when God would send forth His Son, but such was the case.

Antony, although the elder and a practised soldier, was finally overcome by Octavian. Because of Antony's involvement with Cleopatra, queen of Egypt, she persuaded him to stay with her when he should have been away meeting the threat from the young Octavian.

By land and sea Antony's forces were defeated. When he saw that all was lost he slew himself, so that nothing now stood between Octavian and the lordship of the Roman world.

The Romans still abhorred the idea of a king, so on one man were conferred a number of different titles. **Caesar** was a family name which in time was conferred on the next in succession. This is now broadly looked upon as a title equal to that of king. Octavian was then entitled Augustus (meaning honoured, venerable, majestic, worshipful) and with this title went the headships of all the departments of state, secular and religious. It was obvious that to maintain order one man must be in overall command of the Roman armies. This command was invested in **Caesar Augustus** by the title Imperator — or, as we would say, Emperor.

THE FULNESS OF THE TIME

As the hymn of W C Smith says, "Earth was waiting spent and restless, with a mingled hope and fear . . ." "And the oracles were silent, and the prophets were all dead."

Thus on to the world scene appeared Caesar Augustus Imperator.

By this time the rule of Rome had spread over all the lands whose coasts are washed by the Mediterranean Sea, and even kings in far off Asia, although they would not reckon to be subject to Rome, knew that they must obey her.

The question now was, how would this emperor set about the task of ruling this great empire? He had been merciless, cruel, selfish; but a great change came over him, he set aside selfish aims, learnt to curb his fierce temper and with the help of wise counsellors set about establishing the **Pax Augustan**, the Augustan Peace which prevailed over all. It has been said that the doors of the temple of the god of war were closed during this period, as a sign that wars had ceased.

Thus was the stage set for the coming of Emmanuel, God with us, and later, the dissemination of the gospel of "peace on earth, good will toward men" via the Roman roads and a common language.

Perhaps in this can be seen a further meaning of the angel's message, ". . . on earth peace . . ." This prevailed at the time, and from God ". . . good will toward men . . ." Of course the Roman peace was only outward. There cannot be peace in the hearts of men without the Prince of Peace, for "He is our peace", and so when He came peace in the person of the Son of God was upon the earth.

At last we catch up with our opening quotation of Luke 2, "that there went out a decree from Caesar Augustus". It was he who issued the decree that all the world should be taxed. So at the unwitting stroke of a heathen pen was prophecy fulfilled that Christ should be born in Bethlehem of Judea. Perhaps in the future when those simple words are read you will have a new understanding of the movements of God, not only on a great scale in the earth but also in the heart and mind of one man, to accomplish the fulness of the time that His Son should be sent forth.

It is recorded in Matthew 22 vv 15–22 that the Pharisees and the Herodians sought to trap Jesus, saying, "Is it lawful to give tribute unto Caesar or not?" and He said, "Show me the tribute money." They brought Him a penny, and He said to them, "Render therefore unto Caesar the things which are Caesar's, and unto God the things which are God's."

The penny was a silver denarius and the image and superscription thereon that of **Tiberius Caesar**.

At the time of the crucifixion when the Jews declared to Pilate, "We have no king but Caesar," it was to Tiberius that they were referring.

THE CAESARS DEIFIED

The Caesars were now in the process of being deified, as is seen in our next object, which is part of an inscription to **Julia**, the daughter of Augustus. The inscription reads thus: "The people dedicated (this) to the goddess Julia, mother of many children, the daughter of the god Caesar" (BM Inscription 428). Tiberius was obliged to marry Julia after the death of Augustus.

This deification has a bearing on the history of the Church. When persecution arose, Christians were required to sprinkle incense on the flame and to acknowledge Caesar as god with the cry, "Caesar is Lord!"

The Christians upon their baptism would cry, "Jesus is Lord!" Romans 10 v 9: "If thou shalt confess with thy mouth the Lord Jesus" (or, that Jesus is Lord) "and shalt believe in thine heart . . . thou shalt be saved."

This really means that Jesus is God. The Greek work Kurios, superior person or lord, is used in the Septuagint as a translation of the divine tetragrammaton "JHVH" (JEHOVAH), the ineffable name of God. The Christians would know very well what the issue was — acknowledge Caesar as God and deny the Lord Jesus and escape with their life, or confess Jesus as Jehovah and deny Caesar and meet with a horrible death, perhaps thrown to the wild beasts as an entertainment in the arena.

The cruel **Caligula** is our next subject in the line. He reigned for only four years. Herod Agrippa was his friend and companion, and owed his sovereignty to him. This must have been the Caesar to whom Cornelius gave allegiance.

Claudius Caesar (41 AD to 54 AD) is twice mentioned in the Book of Acts. It was prophesied "that there should be a great dearth throughout all the world: which came to pass in the days of Claudius Caesar." And when Paul came to Corinth he "found a certain Jew named Aquila, born in Pontus, lately come from Italy with his wife Priscilla (because that Claudius had commanded all Jews to depart from Rome)."

NERO

It was of **Nero** (54 AD to 68 AD) that the Apostle Paul spoke when he said, "I appeal to Caesar." His true character had not revealed itself in those days. He is well described as "the typical example in history of capricious and inordinate vanity combined with cruelty". The stories of his mad cruelty, which developed soon afterwards, have made him one of the most infamous and notorious of the Caesars. It was truly a fiery trial that the Christians had to pass through in the days of Nero. Accused by him of having set Rome on fire, they were themselves burnt, the stakes being erected in the public gardens of Rome, and the martyrs saturated with inflammable materials, so that the blaze of their burning lit up the dark city. The Christians might have comforted one another then, as Latimer at the stake cheered Ridley many years afterwards, with the prophetic words: "We shall this day light such a candle by God's grace, as I trust shall never be put out."

PAUL THE APOSTLE

Paul's first imprisonment lasted for two years, and he was able to receive all who came to him. To be a Christian was not then punishable with death; but his second imprisonment must have been much more rigorous after the wholesale massacres. Onesiphorus, who was not ashamed of Paul's chain when he was in Rome, had to seek Paul out "very diligently" before he succeeded in finding him, and it was at the risk of his life that he did so. In the same epistle, Paul tells Timothy something about his first appearance before Nero: "At my first answer no man stood with me, but all men forsook me . . . notwithstanding the Lord stood with me, and strengthened me . . . and I was delivered out of the mouth of the lion." It was no private examination, for he says that the strength was given to him, in order that by him "the preaching might be fully known, and that all the Gentiles might hear." We shall never know until the Day shall declare it what was the result of that brave testimony which he soon afterwards sealed with his blood.

The gospel had reached even "Caesar's household". Writing to the Philippians Paul could say, "All the saints salute you, chiefly they that are of Caesar's household." Among the courtiers and attendants of the cruel Nero were some followers of the Lord Jesus. As we look at the sculptured features of the Caesars, it is well to read Romans 16, reminding us of some of those honoured Roman citizens and their households. "Salute them which are of Aristobulus' household . . . Greet them that be of the household of Narcissus which are in the Lord." Mrs Habershon reminds us also of "Pudens and Linus and Claudia, mentioned in the Epistle to Timothy, the last of whom is supposed to have been a British princess."

An interesting sidelight upon practices in the last years of Nero's rule is afforded in Acts 24 vv 26–27. "He (Felix) hoped also that money should have been given him of Paul that he might loose him . . . But after two years **Porcius Festus** came to **Felix'** room: and Felix, willing to show the Jews a pleasure, left Paul bound."

Albinus succeeded Festus as Procurator of Judea, and of him Josephus records in Wars Book 2 chapter 14.1 that, regarding Albinus, "nobody remained in the prisons . . . but he who gave him nothing." Evidently Albinus was not the first one to have this idea, but he did it on a wholesale scale.

CIVIL WAR

Civil war followed the death of Nero and the next Emperor was **Otho**, who ruled only for four months, January–April 69 AD. His sculpture in the BM Catalogue is No 1888.

At this time there were two other contenders for the leadership, Galba with his legions from Spain, and Vitellius, chosen by the armies in Germany.

It became clear that none but a conquering soldier could now grasp the imperial sceptre.

The commander of the army in the East, **Vespasian**, was in the process of a victorious campaign to finally subdue the rebellious Jews of Palestine. He was on his way to besiege Jerusalem and had reached Joppa (Jaffa) when he was declared Emperor by the army. After making sure of support from other armies, he left for Rome and appointed his son Titus as commander.

In an excavation in the old town of Joppa may be seen the remains of a house destroyed by Vespasian when he captured the city while on his way to Jerusalem in 69 AD.

THE JEWS' REVOLT

Here it may be as well to turn aside and consider some events which have bearing upon the gospel before the final destruction of Jerusalem in 70 AD.

In 66 AD the Jews were being pushed towards revolt by events and the implacable fierceness of various revolutionary groups. The Roman General **Cestius**, then president of Syria, marched on Jerusalem to subdue the movements there and to restore order. His army besieged Jerusalem and even got to the temple wall with their heathen standards. The majority of the populace were only too willing to receive the Romans to deliver them from the different factions of the fierce Zealots which controlled the city.

Josephus records of Cestius, "Had he but continued the siege a little longer he had certainly taken the city . . . but . . . he retired from the city without any reason in the world." Whiston, in a footnote, remarks that had Josephus been now a

Christian he might have understood the reason for this inexplicable retreat.

In Matthew 24 vv 15–16 Jesus, in answer to the disciples' question, told them, "When ye therefore shall see the abomination of desolation, spoken of by Daniel the prophet, stand in the Holy Place (whoso readeth, let him understand:) then let them which be in Judea flee into the mountains . . ."; and in Luke 21 vv 20–21, "And when ye shall see Jerusalem compassed with armies, then know that the desolation thereof is nigh. Then let them which are in Judea flee to the mountains; and let them which are in the midst of it depart out; and let not them that are in the countries enter thereinto."

The rebellious parties in Jerusalem had prevented anyone from getting out, so that the mere withdrawal of the Romans would not have allowed the Christians to escape. However, upon the retreat of the Romans the rebels rushed out in pursuit. The Christians, remembering the words of Jesus and seeing the signs, did as He had said and fled from the city to the mountains; thus was the infant Church saved from destruction. In Luke 13 v 5 it is recorded that Jesus said to the people, ". . . Except ye repent, ye shall all likewise perish." It is estimated that some 3 million persons perished, were sold into slavery, or were sent to be thrown to the wild beasts in the arenas of other cities as a result of the siege, fall and destruction of Jerusalem.

JERUSALEM DESTROYED

Mrs Habershon states that whilst the pages of her book were in the press a bust of the Emperor Vespasian was added to the Museum's collection.

After Vespasian we look at the bust of the next emperor, his son **Titus**. As already mentioned, Titus was made commander of the army when his father was declared Emperor and left for Rome.

Prior to his departure for Rome Vespasian had overrun Palestine, including Jericho, leaving Jerusalem isolated. During these operations the settlement of the Essenes by the Dead Sea was destroyed. Of this event we shall hear more later.

Titus spent the winter reorganising his army and in March 70 AD began the assault on Jerusalem. A huge army of four Roman legions with auxiliary troops converged on Jerusalem. On the eve of the Passover Titus appeared before the town's third wall and set up camp on Mt Scopus to the north east.

He caused a stone wall 7,200 metres long to be built around the citadel. No food could reach the people inside and no one could escape. Those who did try to escape were crucified in sight of the city, finally in such numbers that it is recorded that the Romans ran out of wood for stakes to impale people and resorted to the practice of nailing two on a stake, one upside down.

After weeks of famine, disease and internecine strife within the walls, came the final assault. The Antonia tower was taken and destroyed. The last refuge was the temple area and the temple itself. For a week the gates stood firm against the Roman battering rams, then Titus ordered them to be burned.

He had ordered that the temple itself was to be spared, but because of the use the Jews made of the temple precincts in withstanding the invaders, the soldiers disregarded this order and on the tenth of the month Ab (August) 70 AD the temple of Herod crumbled in flames.

The last of the Zealots fought on in the Upper City for another week, but it was hopeless. After five months of bitter siege and fighting the Romans were in complete control of the heaps of ruins that had once been Jerusalem. Part of the Western Wall (Wailing Wall) of the temple area and the three towers of Herod were alone preserved, to provide a garrison for the troops and as a memorial for the city. The remains of the Western Wall and the lower courses of one of the towers, the tower of Phasael, may still be seen today.

Thus was brought about the fulfilment of the words of the Lord Jesus concerning the temple in Matthew 24 v 2, ". . . Verily I say unto you, there shall not be left here one stone upon another, that shall not be thrown down."

In view of the fact that Titus had made it clear that he wished to save the temple, it might reasonably be thought that when all was lost the Jews would have surrendered to save it from destruction. The one factor which brought total disaster upon them was their belief that at the last moment Messiah would come and save them.

PERSECUTION

Domitian succeeded his brother Titus as emperor. He began his reign well enough but turned to evil ways, persecuting the Christians among his other ill deeds. Thus it was that when Domitian in his turn was murdered, there was none to mourn for him. It was probably he who banished the beloved disciple to Patmos, from whence John recorded his Revelation. Chapter 2 v 10 of this book says, "Fear none of those things which thou shalt suffer: behold, the devil shall cast some of you into prison, that ye may be tried; and ye shall have tribulation ten days: be thou faithful unto death, and I will give thee a crown of life." It is of interest to note that Augustine records ten special periods of persecution between the days of Nero and Constantine (64–312 AD). The words of the verse in Revelation 2 were addressed to the Church at Smyrna. **Polycarp**, one-time "Bishop" of Smyrna, was martyred during one of these periods, when he was over 80 years old.

Under **Nerva** the banished Christians were recalled and the Apostle John returned from Patmos. He survived until the reign of **Trajan**. It was by the order of Trajan that **Ignatius** the disciple of John was brought from Antioch to Rome and there thrown to the wild beasts. (When facing the wild beasts in the arena he said, "I am grain of God; let me be ground between the teeth of lions if I may thus become bread to feed God's people.")

New Testament times are covered by the reigns of Caesar Augustus to Trajan.

The wives of two other emperors are represented in the Museum: **Severa**, the wife of **Philip the Elder**, and the wife of **Decius**. Philip was favourable to the Christians and **Jerome** goes so far as to call him a Christian. It is known that he and his wife had been in correspondence with Origen.

The first great general persecution broke out under Decius, but all through most of these reigns Christians were called upon to lay down their lives for the truth. The edict of Nero which made it a capital crime to be a Christian remained unrepealed even in the days of those who may be termed good emperors.

Before leaving the Roman Gallery let us look at the bust of the Emperor **Hadrian**, whom we shall meet again in the Romano-British Gallery later.

After the destruction of Jerusalem in 70 AD it remained just heaps of rubble guarded by the Tenth Roman Legion for some 60 years.

The Emperor Hadrian decided to rebuild Jerusalem as a pagan city, wiping out all memory of Judaism. He called it Aelia Capitolina. Aelia after his own second name, and dedicated to the god Jupiter and goddess Venus of the Capitol in Rome. Above one arch of the Hadrian Gate under the present Damascus Gate in Jerusalem is a defaced inscription which has been deciphered to be the new name of the city.

We have a link in Britain with Hadrian as it was he who built the wall in the North to guard against the Picts and Scots, sections of which may still be seen today.

As we contemplate the Caesars and try to picture the opening scenes of Church history, we see the persecutors on their pedestals and the Church of God trodden under their feet. If we now, from the Entrance Hall, go into the Manuscript Saloon and the King's Library, we shall see evidences of an extraordinary change which has taken place. Here we are surrounded with evidences of a wealthy organisation. Costly books, beautifully illustrated, tell of wealthy monasteries; charters, granted to and by Abbots, tell of the land being in their possession, and now it is the "Church" that has climbed onto the pedestal of power, and in its turn is persecuting the followers of the Lord Jesus. To quote Sir Robert Anderson, "In the days of Pagan Rome the Church was on the side of martyrs. But under Papal Rome the martyrs were the victims of the Church" (*The Bible or the Church*).

Mrs Habershon continues, "In which period is the Church's history most in accordance with the mind and purpose of the great Head of the Church? In the days represented by the portraits in the Roman Gallery, or in the times which brought forth the various manuscripts and documents of the Libraries?"

BRITAIN, THE EMPIRE AND THE CHURCH

Romano-British Antiquities. British Museum Guide pp 178–184. Upper Floor, Room 40.

In this section of the Museum is a bronze statue of the Emperor **Nero**.

Britain was made part of the Roman Empire as a result of the Claudian invasion in 43 AD.

In Philippians 4 v 22 we read of the saints of Caesar's household. This was written from prison in the time of Nero. Statues of the ruling emperor were set up in the Roman Empire so that the people could see a representation of the head of state and pay homage accordingly. We may be certain that there were Christians amongst the soldiers and government officials even as there were in the palace at Rome.

"It is probable that the tidings of the Son of Man crucified and raised again during the reign of the Emperor Tiberius, later spread through these islands more rapidly than the dominion of the emperors, and that before the end of the second century, Christ was worshipped by not a few beyond the wall of Hadrian. In about 200 AD **Tertullian** wrote, 'Parts of Britain were inaccessible to the Romans but have yielded to Christ.' In these mountains, forests and Western Isles on which the Roman Eagles had never swooped, even there the name of Christ was known and honoured.

"The names of three British martyrs have survived from the savage Diocletian persecution towards the end of the third century AD: **Alban** of Verulam, **Aaron** (an otherwise unknown Christian) and **Julius** of Caerleon" (*The Reformation in England*, Merle D'Aubigne).

The idea is abroad and propagated that Christianity was brought to these islands by **Augustine**, the first Archbishop of Canterbury. In the summer of 597 AD Augustine, in a party of 41 missionaries sent out by the Roman Church, landed on the Isle of Thanet. They celebrated their worship in an old ruinous chapel at Canterbury where British Christians had in former times worshipped (D'Aubigne, Vol 1, p 35.) This fact alone is enough to show that there were Christians in England long before the arrival of the emissaries of the Bishop of Rome.

In the gallery of this department is a colossal bronze head of the Emperor Hadrian found in the Thames at London Bridge, and an arm found elsewhere in London. This statue probably stood in Central London. It may have been made to commemorate Hadrian's visit to London in 122 AD, and its dismemberment the work of raiders in late Roman times.

THE MILDENHALL TREASURE

The next thing here to claim our attention is the Mildenhall Treasure, a most impressive set of silver tableware which was ploughed up at Mildenhall in Suffolk during the Second World War. The treasure consists of 34 superb pieces — dishes, cups, bowls, spoons and ladles. These pieces were buried in the middle of the fourth century AD. Looking at this treasure we leap over the years from the primitive Church to the Byzantine era.

The most magnificent item is the great dish. This is decorated in relief with Bacchanalian figures on the outer frieze, sea nymphs on the backs of sea monsters on the inner frieze and a dominating figure, possibly Neptune, in the centre of the dish. In contrast to these pagan scenes, three of the spoons bear evidence of Christianity, being decorated with the Chi-Rho monogram comprising the first letters of Christ's name in Greek, inscribed between the Greek letters Alpha and Omega.

In this treasure we begin to see the answer to Mrs Habershon's question quoted earlier, "What has happened to bring about this great change?" What has happened is that Christianity has now been embraced as the official religion of the Roman Empire — no longer in its primitive purity however, but mixed with pagan myths and superstition.

At the head of the main stairs may be found the mosaic pavement discovered at Hinton St Mary, Dorset, in 1963, where it covered the floors of two rooms of a villa. In the centre is the earliest known representation of Christ, portrayed and executed in mosaic on a floor from the Roman Empire. Behind the head is the Chi-Rho monogram. Another part of the mosaic portrays Bellerophon, mounted on his horse Pegasus, killing the Chimaera, and hunting scenes. Here again is an example of the admixture of Christianity and paganism.

The Emperor **Constantine**, who first moved towards Christianity officially, having gained control of the empire, made his capital Byzantium on the shores of the Bosphorus, instead of Rome, and called it Constantinople.

This opened the way for the rise to power of the Bishop of Rome and a fulfilment of the prophecy in 2 Thessalonians 2 v 7 as seen at the Reformation by the Reformers. About the middle of the nineteenth century another interpretation arose, largely disseminated by J Nelson Darby and the Schofield Bible, which took this prophecy out of its historical setting and put it into a future "dispensation" when the Church and the Holy Spirit would have left the earth.

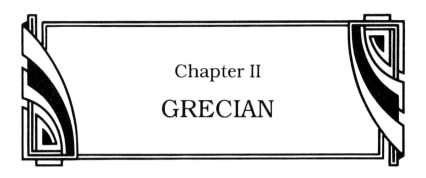

Chapter II
GRECIAN

As we move into the Grecian Antiquities section of the Museum we step further into the world of the New Testament, the world of the Acts and the Epistles.

Before proceeding further, a quotation from W F Albright seems appropriate both for that period and our own.

NEW TESTAMENT TIMES

"The most profound transformation was intellectual, though there were many striking changes in material civilisation. Six centuries of philosophical discussion had accustomed intelligent persons, barbarians as well as Greeks, to think along superficially logical lines and to employ abstract concepts in any discussion. The straightforward empirical wisdom of Elijah's time had too often in fact, been displaced by the rotund phrases of the dialectician. It had now become easy to use education to conceal wisdom and easier still to cover up one's real designs by specious rhetoric" (*The Archaeology of Palestine*. Reprint Penguin 1949).

THE ELGIN MARBLES

Moving into the Duveen Gallery, Room 8 on the current B M Plan, we step back some 1900 years to view some of the very objects on which the Apostle Paul looked during his second missionary journey, for here displayed are sculptured remains from the Parthenon in Athens.

As the apostle waited at Athens for **Silas** and **Timothy**, "his spirit was stirred in him, when he saw the city wholly given to idolatry" (Acts 17 v 16).

During this waiting time the apostle would have had opportunity to explore the city, the chief attraction of which would have been the mighty temple of Athene, the patron goddess of Athens, the **Parthenon**, situated on the Acropolis hill.

As we walk around the remains of the North Frieze, the South Frieze and West Pediments studying the sculptures which represent the ultimate achievement of man in this art form, we get some idea of why the apostle's spirit was "stirred within him".

In these and adjoining rooms we see something of the multiplicity of gods worshipped in the Graeco-Roman world. On the Parthenon frieze is a sculptured representation of the four-yearly procession to escort a new robe for the statue of Athene. Amongst the figures represented are groups of gods and goddesses supposed to be present. Also around us are representations of Ares the god of war, Iris the winged messenger, Zeus and Hera, Athene patron goddess of Athens, Hephaistos god of crafts, Apollo, Artemis (Diana), Helios in his chariot drawn by four horses, Demeter goddess of the corn-bearing earth and her daughter Persephone, Hebe cup-bearer of Zeus, Hestia goddess of earth, Aphrodite goddess of love, her mother Dione, Thalassa the sea in the lap of Gaia the earth, Selene goddess of the moon, Erichthonios son of the god Hephaistos with a snake's tail growing from his body. Surely no more is needed to give the reason why the Apostle's spirit was stirred within him.

He also saw one altar not represented here which he used as a starting point in his speech to the Areopagites when they desired to know of his teaching. This was the altar to the Unknown God. The apostle said, "He whom you ignorantly worship, Him declare I unto you." They listened up to the point where he spoke of the resurrection from the dead and then dismissed him, "but some believed."

To begin his speech the apostle said, "Ye men of Athens, I perceive that in all things ye are too superstitious" (Acts 17 v 22). A marginal reading for the word "superstitious" is "religious". How much of "religion" is just superstition and not a real knowing of God?

The Parthenon could be seen from Mars' Hill where the Areopagus met, so that as the apostle spoke we can imagine him pointing to the temples on the Acropolis as he said, "God

The Parthenon (Model) Athens

Sculpture from East Frieze of The Parthenon: A new robe for
the Statue of Athene is handed to one of her child attendants

18

dwelleth not in temples made with hands" (Acts 17 v 24), and again later, "We ought not to think that the Godhead is like unto gold or silver or stone, graven by art or man's device" (Acts 17 v 29). How appropriate when spoken from where the Parthenon would be in view, with its amazing sculptures — the peak of art and man's device! Almost as amazing is the fact that today in the British Museum in London, 1900 years later, we can look upon some of those very examples of "art and man's device" which the apostle would have seen and of which he was speaking.

THE PARTHENON

The reader may wonder how these marvels came to be in the Museum; a note of this may be worthwhile.

The three chief tribes of the Hellenes were the Ionians, the Dorians and the Aeolians. From the first two derived the names of the styles of architecture known as Ionic and Doric. In time, as the Hellenes became masters of the Mediterranean, the colonies which were founded came to be called the Greater Hellas or Greece.

The chief Ionian state was Athens, with the country round called Attica. It was for control of this area that the legendary contest between Poseidon and Athene took place. Athene being the victor, the city was called Athens.

The original temples on the hill called the Acropolis were destroyed by the Persians in c 480 BC. After the war with the Persians, the Athenians under Pericles, with the architect Ictinos and the sculptor Phidias, began the work of restoration, one of the results of which was the Parthenon, dedicated in 438 BC as a building "of the purest Doric style".

On the Acropolis were three statues of Athene, a wooden one supposed to have fallen from heaven, an enormous bronze one 70 feet high that sailors at sea could see and salute, and a gorgeous gold and ivory one 40 feet high housed in the Parthenon. Regarding the claim concerning the wooden image of Athene, in Acts 19 v 35 there is a similar claim made of the statue of Diana (Artemis) at Ephesus where the townclerk says that everyone knows that the image of the great goddess Diana "fell down from Jupiter".

For a thousand years the Parthenon remained a temple of the goddess Athene Parthenos. For another thousand years it was used as a Christian church, and then as a Turkish mosque.

During the Turkish period it was used as an arsenal, and in 1687 a huge explosion brought down the roof and upper parts. For many years the ruins lay deteriorating, until early in the nineteenth century Lord Elgin funded an expedition to bring to London a great part of the surviving sculptures from the Frieze, Pediments and Metopes, to save them from further damage. For this reason the collection is known as the Elgin Marbles.

In the South Slip Room adjacent to Room 8 is a model of the Parthenon which we should not miss seeing.

The Parthenon was built entirely of marble in the Doric style. It was 228 feet long, 101 feet broad and 65 feet high, surrounded by a peristyle of 46 pillars. Parts of the inside were enlivened with patterns in bright colours; a reproduced sample is on view in the main exhibition. The inside was divided into two chambers, in one of which stood the statue of Athene by Phidias in ivory and gold, the whole amply justifying the apostle's reference to "art and man's device".

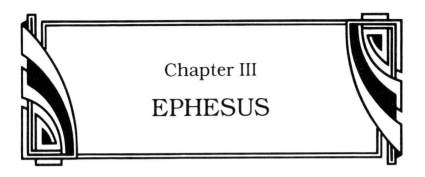

Chapter III
EPHESUS

In Acts 18 v 1 we read that Paul departed from Athens and came to Corinth, and then in Acts 19 v 1 that Paul having passed through the upper coasts came to Ephesus.

Mrs Habershon, in her book of 1909, says that in an ante-room prior to the Ephesus Room are "a number of Greek statuettes, the earliest dating from two or three centuries BC. Amongst them is a representation of a Virgin and Child (which is a striking illustration of the fact that such worship was prominent in many of the heathen religions long before the birth of the Lord Jesus in Bethlehem)." As the exhibits are no longer arranged as in her day, to see these statuettes now we have to move to an upper floor of the Museum, to Room 68 on the plan, Greek and Roman Bronzes and Terracottas. In this section, in a case labelled BOEOTIA 470–330 BC, is exhibited No 820, Goddess With Baby c 450 BC, said to be from Thebes.

This is indeed "a striking illustration" of the carry over of heathen superstition which became mingled with the Christianity of Constantine in the fourth century AD.

Of course the worship of the creature rather than the creator and the turning from pure spirituality to corruption began long before Constantine.

THE TOWER OF BABEL

In the Book of Genesis, immediately after the fall of man we have the first promise of the Saviour. Also in Genesis, after the Flood we have the beginning of all false religion and idolatry. The story of the Tower of Babel is related in Genesis 11 vv1–9. Verse 4 reads thus: "And they said one to another, Go to, let us build us a city and a tower, whose top may reach unto heaven . . ." In the Authorised Version of the Bible the words "may reach" are in italics, showing that they are not in the original, so this should read "whose top unto heaven". The late Rev L T Pearson would quote from an inscription of Nebuchadnezzar, that great builder in brick, which told how he restored the tongue tower and put its top back to its original purpose, astrological.

In the book *Through the Land of Babylonia* by the Rev L T Pearson MA, on pages 28–29 we read, "When Sir Henry Rawlinson excavated at Birs Nimrud, he found inscriptions left by Nebuchadnezzar which are indeed helpful and explanatory: 'The house of the earth's base, the most ancient monument of Babylon I built and finished. I exalted its head with bricks covered with copper . . . the house of the seven lights (the planets) a former king 42 ages ago built but did not complete its head.'"

The Bible says that "the heavens declare the glory of God and the firmament showeth his handiwork." God has written in the stars the gospel story. This has been corrupted by man in the signs of the Zodiac and Greek mythology. The Virgin Mary becomes the Queen of Heaven and is venerated accordingly.

"No astronomer is an astrologer and no astrologer is an astronomer" (Rev L T Pearson MA).

Astrology is a system of foretelling the future, based on the belief that the movements of the stars determine the course of events. It was born in the lands of the Euphrates where the stars and constellations were worshipped as divine, but belief in the divine powers of the stars was current among the Babylonians, Assyrians, Chaldeans and Egyptians, and by the fourth century BC in Greece as well.

The Babylonians associated the stars with the gods themselves, the sign for a god in ancient writing being a star. The planet Venus was identified with Astarte and the planet Mars with Nergal the Babylonian god of death. We still call the planets by the names of Graeco-Roman gods. A standard work on astrology was constructed by the Babylonians as early as the sixteenth century BC. Their observations of signs in the heavens were translated into astrological theories for the foretelling of future events.

In Isaiah 47 v 13 we read, "Thou art wearied in the multitude of thy counsels. Let now the astrologers, the stargazers, the monthly prognosticators, stand up and save thee from these things that shall come upon thee." This verse mentions three distinct groups of professional astrologers among the Assyrians and Babylonians, those who divide the heavens, stargazers and monthly prognosticators. "Those who divide the heavens" suggests the methods used by the astrologers who sectioned the firmament and assigned a particular meaning to each section. Stargazers, another type of astrologer, had detailed tables listing the gathering of the stars and their significance. Monthly prognosticators were sages who read divine omens from the appearance of the new moon. A big "book" on astrology by one Sargon of Akkad was written before 2,000 BC. The twelve equal signs of the Zodiac, as named today, date from a later time and have survived the millennia.

Astronomy is the scientific investigation of the movements of heavenly bodies. Babylonian astronomy developed particularly from the need for adjusting the calendar.

The Greeks took over the Babylonian notion that the stars were gods, and the Greek mythological names for the stars are used to this day.

All these things are condemned in the Bible: "There shall not be found among you anyone . . . that useth divination, or an observer of times, or an enchanter, or a witch, or a consulter with familiar spirits, or a wizard, or a necromancer. For all that do these things are an abomination unto the Lord . . ." (Deuteronomy 18 vv 10–12a).

In our day it seems that pure religion is being driven out and materialism, superstition and idolatrous practices are sweeping in like a flood. However, we have an anchor in the Word of God: "When the enemy shall come in like a flood, the Spirit of the Lord shall lift up a standard against him." Satan can only go as far as God allows.

THE TEMPLE OF DIANA

We move on to Room 12, the Mausoleum Room. In this area is the sculptured base of the column from the temple of Diana at Ephesus, which was actually in place when the apostle and his companions were in that city.

The temple of Diana was one of the seven wonders of the ancient world. It had three rows of 8 columns on the west or main front, two rows of 21 columns on the flanks and two rows of 9 at the rear. These columns rose to almost 60 feet in height. The platform on which they stood measured some 365 by 168 feet, equal to an area of nearly one and a half acres. According to Pliny, 36 of the columns were decorated with sculpture, a most unusual feature.

The story of the discovery of the site and remains of this great temple of Diana is a fascinating one. On behalf of the British Museum, J T Wood carried out excavations on the site of ancient Ephesus from 1869 to 1874, but found no trace of the temple mentioned in the Book of Acts. In the last year of his activities he discovered an inscription describing the route of a procession carrying certain valuable pieces made in honour of Diana. This route was described as going to the temple via one gate and returning by another. Wood realised that if these gates could be identified he would be on the way to discovering the location of the temple. He was able to do this and the evidence pointed to a swamp covered by silt from the river Cayster. Digging here in the last year of his expedition and with money running out, he made the triumphant discovery of what we see before us, the sculptured base of a column of the temple of Diana.

At Ephesus Paul "spoke boldly in the synagogue for the space of three months, disputing and persuading the things concerning the kingdom of God. But when divers were hardened and believed not, but spake evil of that way before the multitude, he departed from them and joined by the disciples he disputed daily in the school of Tyrannus. This continued for about two years; so that all they which dwelt in Asia heard the word of the Lord Jesus, both Jews and Greeks" (Acts 19 vv 8–10). "So mightily grew the word of God and prevailed" (Acts 19 v 20).

Paul then sent two of those who ministered unto him into Macedonia, but he himself stayed in Ephesus. During this time "there arose no small stir about that way". (Believers in the Lord Jesus were called people of The Way.) In Acts 19 v 24 to the end, we read of the incident concerning the temple and the goddess Diana which followed.

There were in Ephesus silversmith craftsmen who made their wealth producing silver shrines for Diana. These would be sold, even as such things are at various places in our day, to the

Excavations and Theatre at Ephesus

Temple of Diana: Column Base

great numbers of worshippers coming to the temple. In modern times such people would be called tourists or pilgrims.

One Demetrius called a meeting of his fellow craftsmen and said to them that, "This Paul hath persuaded and turned away much people, saying that they be no gods, which are made with hands: so that not only this our craft is in danger to be set at nought; but also that the temple of the great goddess Diana should be despised, and her magnificence destroyed, whom all Asia and the world worshippeth."

On hearing this they were furious and cried out saying, "Great is Diana of the Ephesians." Such a stir was caused that the whole city was filled with confusion, and having caught two of Paul's travelling companions they rushed with one accord into the theatre. One of Paul's friends tried to speak to the people, but when they discovered that he was a Jew, they continued for about two hours chanting, "Great is Diana of the Ephesians!"

The authorities were greatly concerned at this riotous assembly. When the townclerk at last obtained a hearing he told them that there was no danger at all to Diana or her worship, and that if Demetrius and his fellow craftsmen had a matter against anyone, "the law is open, and there are deputies: let them implead one another", and he dismissed the assembly.

Here in the Mausoleum Room, the life-size figures on this column drum represent Hermes, the 'messenger of the gods with his herald's staff, the winged figure of death and what is thought to be Alcestis, who in mythology volunteered to sacrifice her own life to save that of her husband, but was allowed to return from the underworld.

The original temple was burned down in 356 BC by one Herostratus who hoped thereby to obtain fame. This, reputedly, was done on the night of Alexander the Great's birth. Rebuilding started soon afterwards and was in progress some twenty years later when Alexander visited Ephesus and offered to bear the cost of completing it. The new temple was essentially the same plan as the old one.

In AD 262 it was sacked and burnt by the Goths, but rebuilt afterwards to some extent. It would have continued in use until AD 380 when the Emperor Theodosius ordered the closing of all pagan temples. Much of the fabric was robbed in the sixth century AD to build the Cathedral of

St John Theologos on a neighbouring hill. Thus even the very stones bear silent witness to the mixture of the old idol worship with Christianity.

What a difference between these imaginary figures of heathen myth and the solid historical foundation of the Bible record, exemplified by this sculptured column drum from the temple of Diana of the Ephesians.

H V Morton in his book *In the Steps of St Paul*, as he sat gazing at the ruins and waste that had been Ephesus, wrote, "I remembered these words from the Revelation: 'Unto the angel of the church of Ephesus write; these things saith He that holdeth the seven stars in His right hand, who walketh in the midst of the seven golden candlesticks . . . I have somewhat against thee, because thou hast left they first love. Remember therefore from whence thou art fallen and repent, and do the first works; or else I will come unto thee quickly, and will remove thy candlestick out of his place . . .

"I looked towards the tamarisk bushes, I listened for the bittern's call, I heard the chorus of frogs in the marshes. Truly the candlestick of Ephesus has been removed out of its place."

After all Demetrius was right; the temple of Diana disappeared and the remains were buried in mud, but the gospel which Paul preached endures indestructible.

In the recently opened (1985) Wolfson Galleries in the Basement of the Museum are displayed many pieces from Ephesus, together with large photographs of the excavations there.

Alexander The Great   Photograph: BM

Roman Portraits in Wolfson Gallery — Nero is fourth from right in the top row

Chapter IV

ALEXANDER THE GREAT

On leaving the Ephesus Room, there was in former times on the right hand side of the door a bust of **Alexander the Great**. This is no longer to be seen there. It is at present on view amongst the Roman emperors, but it cannot be said what its final position will be. Has Alexander any connection with the Bible? The answer is, yes, and of great interest too.

In the Book of Daniel, chapter 8, we read of a vision which Daniel had when at the palace of Belshazzar at Shushan. He saw a ram standing by the river Ulai. This ram had two horns, which were high, but one was higher than the other and came up last. He saw the ram pushing west, north and south so that none could stand against him, but he did just what he liked and became great.

As Daniel was considering this, a he-goat came from the west on the face of the whole earth, and touched not the ground. In other words the goat was so furious and unimpeded in his progress that we might say he was jet propelled. The goat had a notable horn between his eyes. He came to the ram that had two horns, and rushed on him in the fury of his power, and was moved with choler against the ram and broke his two horns and smote him. The ram was powerless before him and was cast to the ground and stamped upon, and none could deliver the ram.

The goat waxed very great: and when he was strong, the great horn was broken; and for it came up four notable ones toward the four winds of heaven.

From verses 20–25 Daniel is given the interpretation of the vision. "The ram which thou sawest having two horns are the kings of Media and Persia, and the rough goat is the king of Grecia; and the great horn between his eyes is the first king.

Now that being broken, whereas four stood up for it, four kingdoms shall stand up out of the nation, but not in his power . . ." This is as far as we need to go for our purpose. The rest of the prophecy concerns **Antiochus Epiphanes** of later date.

The great horn of the rough goat was Alexander the Great, and the four notable horns which came up after the great horn was broken, are the four generals between whom the empire of Alexander was divided after his death, **Ptolemy, Seleucid, Lysimachus** and **Antigonus**.

Alexander was the son of **Philip** the Second of Macedonia, born at Pella in 356 BC. At the age of 16 he was entrusted with the government when his father marched against Byzantium.

Following the murder of Philip, Alexander became king of Macedonia at the age of 20 and found himself surrounded by enemies. He first put down rebellion in his own kingdom and then rapidly marched into Greece. His unexpected activity overawed the opposition and he was elected commander against the Persians. He then directed his arms against the Barbarians in the north and advanced as far as the Danube, which he crossed.

A report of his death having reached Greece, the Thebans once more took arms. Alexander advanced into Boeotia by rapid marches, took Thebes by assault, destroyed all the buildings with the exception of the house of Pindar, killed most of the inhabitants and sold the rest as slaves. (Pindar was a famous Greek poet.)

In the spring of 334 BC he crossed the Hellespont with about 35,000 men. At Ilium he offered sacrifice to Athene, placed garlands on the tomb of Achilles and himself ran round it.

Alexander's first engagement with the Persians was on the river Granicus in Mysia (May 384 BC) where he won a signal victory. This battle was followed by the capture or submission of the chief towns on the west coast of Asia Minor.

He marched along the coast of Lycia and Pamphylia and then north into Phrygia and to Gordium, where he cut or untied the celebrated Gordian Knot, which it was said was only to be loosened by the conqueror of Asia.

From Gordium he marched through the centre of Asia Minor into Cilicia, where he nearly lost his life at Tarsus by a fever.

Darius in the meantime had collected an army of some 60,000 men, whom Alexander defeated in the narrow plain of Issus. Darius escaped across the Euphrates but his mother, wife and children fell into the hands of Alexander, who treated them with respect.

Alexander now directed his arms against the cities of Phoenicia, most of which submitted, but Tyre was taken only after an obstinate defence of seven months.

After marching through the country, Gaza was besieged and fell after two months.

Alexander then marched into Egypt which willingly surrendered to him, for the Egyptians had always hated the Persians. At the beginning of 331 BC at the mouth of the west branch of the Nile he founded the city of Alexandria.

In the same year he set out to meet Darius, who had collected another army. He marched through Phoenicia and Syria to the Euphrates, which he crossed at the ford of Thapsacus. There he proceeded through Mesopotamia, crossed the Tigris and at length met with the immense hosts of Darius in the plains of Gaugamela. The battle, fought in the month of October 331 BC, ended in the complete defeat of the Persians. Thus did the noble horn of the rough goat, Alexander, destroy the ram and shatter his two horns, the kingdoms of the Medes and Persians.

Alexander was now the conqueror of Asia and began to adopt Persian habits and customs. He marched to Babylon, Susa and Persepolis, all of which surrendered to him. At Susa he found a great treasure and, among other spoils originally carried off by **Xerxes** (the Ahasuerus of Esther), the statues of Harmodius and Aristogeiton, which he sent back to Athens.

At the beginning of 330 BC Alexander marched from Persepolis into Media, to Ecbatana, in pursuit of Darius whom he followed into Parthia, where Darius was murdered. Alexander sent his body back to Persepolis to be buried in the tombs of the Persian kings.

After campaigning in India, Alexander returned to Susa at the beginning of 325 BC. He had great schemes for making the Tigris and the Euphrates navigable. His plan was to make Babylon his capital. On his return to Babylon he was attacked by a fever and died after an illness of eleven days, in May or June 323 BC, at the age of 33.

FOUR NOTABLE ONES

After his death the empire was divided between four of his generals, Ptolemy, Seleucid, Lysimachus and Antigonus, the four "notable ones" of Daniel's prophecy.

In the above account many names of places and people mentioned in the Old and New Testaments occur: Macedonia, Pamphilia, Phrygia, Cilicia and of course Tarsus, the home city of the apostle Paul, Phoenicia, Tyre, Egypt, Syria, Mesopotamia, Susa, Media, Persia, Parthia, India, Babylon and the river Euphrates.

Does all this have any relevance for us today? It certainly does, because it shows that God is sovereign over the nations and confirms the certainty of the fulfilment of the Word of God.

Wherever Alexander went he took the Greek culture and language. "As early as the third century BC, Greek became the principal language of the Jews even in their religious services" (*Pictorial Biblical Encyclopedia*). At Alexandria the Hebrew Scriptures and other Jewish writings were translated into Greek. "During the Hellenistic period Greek superseded Aramaic as the predominant language used for literature as well as everyday speech. This universality had a great influence on other languages and made the dissemination of Greek culture all the easier" (*Pictorial Biblical Encyclopedia*, Cornfeld). "Even after the Roman conquest Greek continued in use, the Romans themselves using it as their administrative language in the Middle East. The Greek of this era was a uniform language, local dialects being almost unknown. It was called 'Koine' (the universal) and in this the Septuagint and the New Testament were written" (*Pictorial Biblical Encyclopedia*, Cornfeld).

It is of interest to note this authoritative statement regarding "Koine". The impression has been given that this was a common Greek used by the working class people. It certainly was not the Classical Greek of literature, but a universal form used for administrative purposes and also generally. In all this we see the way being prepared for when "in the fulness of time, God sent forth His Son."

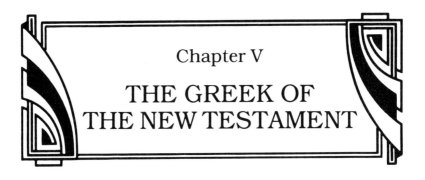

Chapter V

THE GREEK OF
THE NEW TESTAMENT

"During the past half-century papyrologists have been active, and a great many previously obscure words and grammatical usages in the Greek New Testament have proved to be excellent Koine, that is, Greek as employed by ordinary men all over the Greek speaking world of that day. At first the enthusiasm of scholars like Adolph Deissmann, who became the leader of this new branch of research, carried the day; IT BECAME COMMON BELIEF THAT NEW TESTAMENT GREEK WAS THE ORDINARY VERNACULAR OF THE FIRST CENTURY AD and that the striking divergences between it and authors like Diodorus or Plutarch or like Philo and Josephus, were due simply to the fact that the writers of the New Testament were unlettered men.

"BUT THIS WAS SIMPLY NOT TRUE; there remained a big difference between the Greek of the New Testament and the language of the letters and business documents of unlettered Greeks in Egypt.

"Arthur Darby Nock, one of the foremost living authorities on the period, wrote recently, 'There has been much exaggeration of the Koine element in the New Testament.'

"As long as the Greek of the New Testament remained unparalleled because of the lack of any writings except sophisticated literary works like Philo and Plutarch from the period of Jesus and the apostles, it was hard to arrive at any objective conclusion.

"Now it became evident that there must really have been strong Hebrew and Aramaic influence on the New Testament Greek in order to explain the apparent Semitisms in the New Testament as contrasted with Koine. After all, the writers of the New Testament (including almost certainly Luke) were Jews, and Aramaic was their mother tongue. It had commonly been supposed that it was a lack of native command of Greek and of a Hellenic education which prevented the writers of the New Testament from writing in good Greek.

"Such scholars as C F Burney and C C Torrey, following occasional hints by earlier students, maintained that much of the Gospels and the Acts had been translated from written Aramaic sources. In other words, they held that the Semitic colouring was not due to lack of education on the part of ancient writers, but was rather the outcome of too great fidelity to the Aramaic original which they were translating. Torrey was a first class authority on Aramaic and a very well trained philologian" (*The Archaeology of Palestine*, W F Albright pp 198–199).

Albright again: "Other evidence makes it increasingly probable that the Aramaic element in the Gospels comes from the translation of orally transmitted documents, that is, oral Aramaic records of the words and doings of Jesus. When we recall the extent to which oral transmission of the words of the Rabbis was emphasized in contemporary and later Jewish schools, such handing down by word of mouth seems only reasonable. Christians may thus continue to read the Greek Gospels without apprehending serious errors in translation" (*The Archaeology of Palestine* p 203).

There can be no difficulty whatever about the above to one who believes in the divine inspiration of the Scriptures. Scholars would have us believe that things are much more complicated than they really are, but faith moves mountains. The words of the Lord Jesus are very relevant here: "Say unto this mountain, Be thou removed, and be thou cast into the sea; it shall be done." It is almost hilarious — these philological mountains can be removed and cast into the depths of the sea, and not by what is called "blind faith" either!

If we will but go to the Word itself the problem disappears. All concerned have a great regard for W F Albright, but even he seems to miss the obvious, for in John 14 v 26 the Lord Jesus says, "But the Comforter, which is the Holy Ghost, whom the Father will send in my name, he shall teach you all things, and bring all things to your remembrance, whatsoever I have said unto you." Therefore why speak of an "oral tradition" as though handed on to others, when the writers themselves were thinking and remembering in Aramaic? Even if, as generally supposed, the apostle Peter was dictating to Mark when writing the Gospel of Mark, the same thing would apply, for Peter would have been thinking and speaking in Aramaic.

In that one verse in John is shown the combined operation of the Godhead in Trinity — Father, Son and Holy Spirit.

The words which follow in verse 27 have much relevance: "Peace I leave with you, my peace I give unto you: not as the world giveth, give I unto you. Let not your heart be troubled, neither let it be afraid." We can indeed have complete confidence in and be at peace about the Bible which has been handed down to us, despite the emendations of the modern versions throwing doubt on the veracity of the Word of God.

It is of interest to note that Albright is of the firm opinion that the Gospel of John was the earliest of the Gospels to be written and not the latest as is so widely taught today. He is certain that the whole of the New Testament, as we have it, was extant in the lifetime of the Apostles.

The Church of the Lord Jesus is built upon Himself, the Rock, but the revelation of this came by the spoken word of Peter: "Thou art the Christ, the Son of the Living God." This word came not by Peter but by revelation from God Himself.

We need to lay foundations on the Rock Himself who is the Living Word; but let us beware lest we build with materials of subtle unbelief which finally will be swept away in the all consuming fire of God, although we ourselves may be saved, albeit with loss. Let us rather be like the man "which built an house, and digged deep, and laid the foundation on a rock" (Luke 6 v 48). Sand can never provide a sure foundation, no matter how deep one digs.

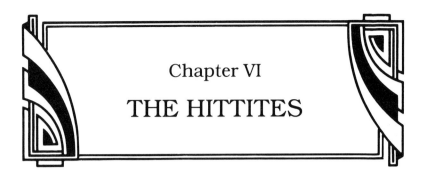

Chapter VI
THE HITTITES

"And the **Hittites**, and the Perizzites, and the Rephaims" (Genesis 15 v 20). The Hittites were descendants of Heth, son of Canaan: this mysterious people who for many years were thought never to have existed. Not many years ago textual critics of the Bible, the so-called "higher critics", were actually saying that the mention of such a people was proof of the inaccuracy of the Bible record and showed its unhistorical basis. They themselves knew nothing of the Hittites, therefore the Hittites could not have existed.

This type of statement was typical of the unbelieving scholars of the period. In 1869, the great Semitic scholar Professor Noldeke published a treatise on "The Unhistorical Character of the Fourteenth Chapter of Genesis". He declared that "criticism" had for ever disproved its claims to be historical. Note the phrase "for ever". He claimed that "the names of the princes in it were etymological inventions."

This was in 1869. By 1903 criticism was "discreetly silent about the conclusions which it had announced with such assurance. In the interval the excavator and archaeologist had been at work and the ancient world of Western Mesopotamia had risen again from the grave of centuries. The increase of knowledge has not been favourable to the results of 'criticism'. It has proved them to be nothing but the baseless fabric of subjective imagination" (A H Sayce). What a statement, coming from the then Professor of Assyriology at Oxford University himself, at one time on the side of the "critics" but completely convinced otherwise by the results of Biblical Archaeology.

The same spirit of unbelief is still abroad today. Listening to eminent scholars speaking on the Bible, one is struck by the phrases used so often: "Of course this is only theory," "There

A Hittite monument showing the strange hieroglyphics which have not yet been deciphered

Photograph: BM

are three theories regarding this; I will take the middle one," and so on. Prophecy is completely denied on the grounds that because of its accuracy it could only possibly have been written after the event. Professor Sayce's comment still stands: "It is only where the evidence is imperfect . . . that the theoretical side of the fact assumes undue proportions, and renders the fact provisional only. It is archaeology and not philology that has to do with history." So far as the historical side of the question is concerned the philologist pure and simple is ruled out of court. "However, criticism has endeavoured to bolster up the weakness of the philological method by an appeal to the doctrine of evolution. When we are told that the development of religious ideas in Israel or elsewhere must have followed certain lines, we need only point to the archaeological discoveries which have shattered similarly subjective theories of the development in Egypt and the early Greek world."

A good example of the wildly differing theories arising from philological analysis of the Pentateuch may be seen in the *Lion Handbook to the Bible* on page 214, "The Cities of the Conquest" by Professor Alan Millard, Rankin Senior Lecturer in Hebrew and Ancient Semitic Languages in the University of Liverpool. "Many scholars have explained Israel's possession of the promised land in terms of a gradual infiltration by nomadic herdsmen. Or they see it as a combination of infiltration and a movement of a few tribal groups from Egypt, perhaps on more than one occasion and over several generations. Or they even envisage a general revolt of the people of the land."

These widely varying opinions are all connected with theories involving the documentary analysis of the Pentateuch. These assign stories to a number of different sources, so proposing separate origins for them and fostering views of unrelated tribal histories. Closely linked with this is a theory that the concept of Israel as a nation was formed long after the conquest and read back into early times by later Israelite historians. So we can see Professor Sayce's "house of cards" being built on the baseless fabric of subjective imagination, and in the minds of the builders, of no limit, "whose top shall reach unto heaven".

Some of these theories are still extant today and taught as fact in colleges and schools. Professor Sayce remarks, "An edifice reared on the subjective fancies and assumptions of the modern European scholar is necessarily a house of cards."

Where in all this do the Hittites come? Indirectly in being "discovered" they have performed a great service to the Bible-believing people in demonstrating the collapse of the "house of cards" erected by textual critics.

According to Young's *Analytical Concordance of the Bible* there are 46 references to the Hittites in the Old Testament. Among them are the following: Abraham purchased the cave of Machpelah from "the people of the land, even the children of Heth," and from "Ephron the Hittite." Their city "Hebron was built seven years before Zoan in Egypt." We read of Jerusalem, "Thy father was an Amorite and thy mother a Hittite."

Esau married "Judith the daughter of Beeri the Hittite." Abimelech the Hittite and Uriah the Hittite were amongst the followers of king David. Toi king of Hamath, a Hittite city, sent his son Joram with a present of "vessels of silver, and vessels of gold, and vessels of brass," which David dedicated to the Lord.

Solomon had horses and chariots brought out of Egypt for the kings of the Hittites; he "loved many strange women," among them "women of the Hittites."

The incident related in 2 Kings 7 shows that the Hittites were a powerful people, for when the Syrians besieged Samaria and the Lord interfered on behalf of Israel, He "made the host of the Syrians to hear a noise of chariots and a noise of horses, even the noise of a great host: and they said one to another, Lo, the king of Israel hath hired against us the kings of the Hittites and the kings of the Egyptians to come upon us." The Hittites and the Egyptians are thus put in equality with each other, and the Syrians were so smitten with terror that they fled precipitately.

It is likely that the first heathen congregation to which the gospel was preached was of Hittite origin, for in Acts 14 v 11 we read, "When the people saw what Paul had done, they lifted up their voices, saying in the speech of Lycaonia, The gods are come down to us in the likeness of men." Some have held that this was a Hittite dialect.

The **Neo-Hittite Landing**, No 53 on the Museum Plan, houses the sculptures and inscriptions in the strange hieroglyphics of the Hittites. In Room 58, amongst the Nimrud Ivories is an ivory from Charchemish, No 116169, this city being the capital of the Neo-Hittite empire. It is a fragmentary panel with a lion above a rounded moulding, possibly part of an armchair. To get an idea of the appearance of the Hittite we have to go to Room 24 on the ground floor of the Museum, the Ancient Palestine Room. On one wall of this room are casts of ethnic types taken by Sir Flinders Petrie from Egyptian base reliefs. No 1 is of Hittites, taken from the Ramasseum at Western Thebes.

In 2 Chronicles 8 v 7 we read, "As for all the people that were left of the Hittites . . . them did Solomon make to pay tribute." Again, in 2 Kings 7 v 6 we read how the Syrians thought that the king of Israel had hired the "kings of the Hittites" against them.

"At this period the great days of the Hittite empire at the time of Thutmose and Rameses were a thing of the past. Their power had already passed its zenith when Rameses defeated them at Kadesh, but the great disaster occurred when the new invaders, Phrygians, Philistines, etc, carried all before them, leaving the Hittite lands and Northern Syria desolated, and blotted out the memory of the Hittite power that had bound its heterogeneous races together for 1500 years. From then until a few years ago their ancient capital at Hattusas (Boghaz Keui) lay buried in forgotten ruins." So says Stephen L Caiger in his book *Bible and Spade*, 1936.

In an article on the Egyptians by R J Williams in *Peoples of Old Testament Times*, edited by Prof D J Wiseman, OUP 1936, we read thus of Rameses the Second: "In his fifth year, about 1290 BC he set forth against a powerful Syrian coalition formed by Muwatallis the Hittite king. At Kadesh on the Orontes he fell into a clever trap and only with the greatest bravery was able to extricate himself and his troops from probable annihilation." (It was by chance that reinforcements arrived on the scene after his defeat and took the Hittites and Syrians by surprise.) "In characteristic fashion, this was later proclaimed in his royal inscriptions as a glorious victory." This "characteristic" of Rameses the Second could have a bearing on the supposed date of the Exodus, as will be suggested later.

Some extracts from Hittite writings may help to bring alive to us this ancient people who for so long, in the minds of the critics, were thought never to have existed.

Extract from Hittite law:

If anyone hires a plough ox for one month, its hire is one shekel of silver.

If anyone harnesses a yoke of oxen, its hire is one half peck of barley.

40

If anyone steals bees in a swarm, formerly they used to give one mina of silver; now he shall give five shekels of silver.

The following is part of a typical paragraph from a land deed: Estate of Tiwataparas: 1 man, Tiwataparas; 1 boy, Haruwandulis; 1 woman, Azzias; 2 girls, Arrittis and Hantawacas. Total 5 persons.

The deed goes on to enumerate the totals of oxen, sheep, lambs, rams, goats and kids, in all 36 small cattle. 1 house. As pasture for oxen 1 acre of meadow in the town of Parkalla. 3½ acres of vineyard with 82 fruit trees.

Corn, wine and oil represent the staple products of the country, but peas, beans and flax are mentioned.

The Hittites had silver, copper, bronze, lead and iron. By the 13th century BC the people of Asia Minor were pre-eminent in iron smelting.

The medium of exchange in the Hittite kingdom was silver, or for small denominations lead in bars or rings measured by weight.

The units of weight were the shekel and the mina, 40 shekels to one mina. The Babylonian mina equalled 60 shekels and the Hebrew mina 50 shekels.

This brings to mind an interesting sidelight on the writing on the wall in Daniel 5: "Mina, Mina, Shekel, Persia." "Thou art weighed in the balances and found wanting. Thy kingdom is divided (the divided shekel) and given to the Medes and Persians."

Regarding their religion, the god was to his worshippers exactly what a master was to his slaves. He had to be fed, tended, appeased and flattered. Even so, he could not be relied on to be always watching his servants' interests. Part of his time would be spent in amusement, or in travelling, sleeping or attending to business, and at such times his worshippers would call in vain for his help, as did the prophets of Baal on Mount Carmel. There were special ceremonies to entice the missing god back again. This throws light upon the incident of Elijah and the prophets of Baal. They "called on the name of Baal from morning even until noon, saying, 'O Baal, hear us.' But there was no voice, nor any that answered. And it came to pass at noon, that Elijah mocked them and said, 'Cry aloud, for he is a god; either he is talking, or he is pursuing, or he is in a journey, or peradventure he sleepeth and must be awakened.' And they cried aloud and cut themselves after their manner with knives and lancets, till the blood gushed out upon them" (1 Kings 18 vv 26–28).

Before their eclipse the Hittites had founded the city of Carchemish on the Upper Euphrates, and here the "people that were left of them" established another but far less powerful kingdom, hence the title Neo-Hittite. So again the spade of the archaeologist confirms the reliability of the Bible record.

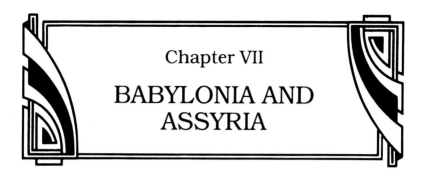

Chapter VII
BABYLONIA AND ASSYRIA

There could hardly be anything more appropriate to begin this section on Babylonia and Assyria than to quote from the preface to the first edition of *Assyria: Its Princes, Priests and People* by Professor A H Sayce:

CUNEIFORM

"Among the many wonderful achievements of the present century (nineteenth) there is none more wonderful than the recovery and decipherment of the monuments of ancient Nineveh. For generations the great oppressing city had slept buried beneath the fragments of its own ruins, its history lost, its very site forgotten. Its name had passed into the region of myth even in the age of the classical writers of Greece and Rome; Ninos or Nineveh had become a hero-king about whom strange legends were told, and whose conquests were fabled to have extended from the Mediterranean to India. Little was known of the history of the mighty Assyrian empire beyond what might be learned from the Old Testament, and that little was involved in doubt and obscurity. Scholars wrote long treatises to reconcile the statements of Greek historians with those of Scripture, but they only succeeded in evolving theories which were contradicted and overthrown by the next writer. There was none so bold as to suggest that the history and life of Assyria was still lying hidden beneath the ground, ready to rise up and disclose its secrets at the touch of a magician's rod. The rod was the spade and the patient sagacity which deciphered and interpreted what the spade had found. It might have been thought that the cuneiform or wedge-shaped inscriptions of Assyria could never be forced to reveal their mysteries. The language in which they were written was unknown, and all clue

43

to the meaning of the multitudinous characters that composed them had long been lost. Nevertheless the great feat was accomplished. Step by step the signification of the cuneiform characters and the words they concealed was made out, until it is now possible to translate an ordinary Assyrian text with as much ease and certainty as a page of the Old Testament.

"The revelation that awaited the decipherer was startling in the extreme. The ruins of Nineveh yielded not only sculptures and inscriptions carved in stone, but a whole library of books. True, the books were written upon clay and not on paper, but they are none the less real books, presenting us with a clear and truthful reflection of Assyrian thought and belief, the life they led and their history as they have told it themselves.

"It is a strange thing to examine for the first time one of the clay tablets of the old Assyrian library. Usually it has been more or less broken by the catastrophe of that terrible day when Nineveh was captured by its enemies, and the palace and library burnt and destroyed together. When the last of the characters upon it were read, it was in the days when Assyria was still a name of terror, and the destruction that God's prophets had predicted was still to come. When its last reader laid it aside, Judah had not as yet undergone the chastisement of the Babylonish exile, the Old Testament was an uncompleted volume, the kingdom of the Messiah a promise of the distant future. We are brought face to face, as it were, with men who were the contemporaries of Isaiah, of Hezekiah, of Ahaz — of men whose names have been familiar to us since we first read the Bible by our mother's side.

SENNACHERIB

"Tiglath-Pileser and Sennacherib can never again be to us mere names. We possess the records which they caused to be written, and in which they told the story of the campaigns in Palestine. The records are not copies of older texts; they are original documents which were recited to the kings who ordered them to be compiled, and who may have held them in their own hands. Never again can the heroes of the Old Testament be to us as lay figures, whose story is told by a voice that comes from a dark and unreal past. The voice has now become a living one, and we can realise that Isaiah and those of whom Isaiah wrote were men of flesh and blood like ourselves.

"One result of the recovery of Assyria was its confirmation of the correctness of the Holy Writ. The later history of the Old Testament no longer stands alone. Once it was itself the sole witness for the truth of the narratives it contains. All is changed now. The earth has yielded up its secrets, the ancient civilisation of Assyria has furnished us with records, the authenticity of which none can deny, which run side by side with those of the Book of Kings, confirming, explaining, and illustrating them. It has been said that just at the moment when sceptical criticism seemed to have achieved its worst, and to have resolved the narratives of the Old Testament into myths or fables, God's Providence was raising up from the grave of centuries a new and unimpeachable witness for the truth. Before the cuneiform monuments were interpreted no one could have suspected that they would have poured such a flood of light upon Old Testament history.

"The Isaianic authorship of the 'burden of Egypt' can never again be denied. Nahum we now can read with a new interest and understanding. The very date of his prophecy, so long disputed, can be fixed approximately by its reference to the sack of No-Amon or Thebes (Nahum 3 v 8).

"The prophecy was delivered hard upon sixty years before the fall of Nineveh, when the Assyrian empire was at the height of its prosperity. Human foresight could little have imagined that so great and terrible a power was so soon to disappear. And yet the very moment when it seemed strongest and most secure, the Jewish prophet was uttering a prediction which the excavations of Botta and Layard have shown to have been carried out literally in fact. Of the words which he pronounced against the doomed city there is none which has not yet come to pass.

"Those who would learn how marvellously the monuments of Assyria illustrate and corroborate the pages of Sacred History, need only to compare the records they contain with the narratives of the Book of Kings. Between the history of the monuments and the history of the Bible there is perpetual contact; and the voice of the monuments is found to be in strict harmony with that of the Old Testament."

In his treatise on "The Unhistorical Character of the Fourteenth Chapter of Genesis", Professor Noldeke stated, "At so distant a date Babylonian armies could not have marched into Canaan, much less could Canaan have been a subject

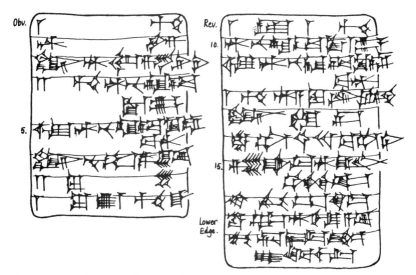

Drawing of Text of Cuneiform Tablet (2049 B.C.): A receipt from the Temple official at Ur in Babylonia. It records offerings of Goats, Oxen and one Lamb from various individuals for three deities. The drawing is by Dr I L Finkel of The British Museum

Hammurabi, King of Babylon (c.1792–1750 B.C.) Photograph: BM

province of Babylonia." He claimed that the whole story was a fiction based upon the Assyrian conquest of Palestine in later days.

The fourteenth chapter of Genesis, verses one to four, records a list of the names of ancient kings. Archaeology has shown that far from being "etymological inventions and a fiction", these kings were very real historical figures, whose names have been illustrated and verified by the cuneiform inscriptions.

To take but one example, that of **Amraphel*, king of Shinar**. Shinar was northern Babylonia where Amraphel reigned, and Amraphel proves to be none other than Hammurabi, the well-attested king of Babylon, for, says Professor Sayce, "the name Hammurabi is letter for letter the Amraphel of Genesis." All the evidence points to the fact that the narrative must have been copied from a written Babylonian record and written in Hebrew as we find it today.

"There is a second conclusion to be deduced from the accuracy with which the names in the Babylonian record have been preserved in the Hebrew text. The fact enhances our opinion of the Hebrew text of the Pentateuch; it cannot be so uncertain or corrupt as it has sometimes been the fashion to believe. Even the proper names contained in it have been handed down correctly. The text must have been transcribed with the same official accuracy as we now know to have been enforced in the case of Babylonian and Assyrian literature.

"In Assyria and Babylonia the work was entrusted to the hands of professional scribes, and the minute care which was bestowed upon the accurate transcription of the texts was extraordinary. On comparing a text compiled for one of the Babylonian libraries of Amraphel with a copy of it made for the library of Nineveh fifteen hundred years later, the differences are slight and unimportant. Indeed the tablets are full of examples of the scrupulous honesty with which the copyists set about the work. The reproduction of the older documents was carried out with almost Masoretic exactitude; we look in vain for that free handling of the original authorities about which the 'higher criticism' has so much to say.

"The literary methods of Babylonia and Assyria were in use also in the schools of Israel and Judah. They were not the methods supposed by the modern critic, but they were

*See footnote on page 68

47

methods consecrated by the usage of centuries wherever the influence of Babylonian culture had penetrated" (*Monument Facts and Higher Critical Fancies*, Professor A H Sayce).

There were seven great monarchs who ruled over Assyria and Babylon who were closely connected with Bible history.

During the nineteenth century much of the sacred record was declared to be myth and most unreliable. This was due to the so-called "higher criticism" emanating originally from Germany. It is passing strange that the land which fostered the Reformation should, within 300 years, produce this faith-destroying attack on the Bible.

However, "when the enemy shall come in like a flood, the Spirit of the Lord shall lift up a standard against him." With the battle raging, Biblical Archaeology began. This was so effective in shattering the false assumptions of the "higher critics" that one of their number, Professor A H Sayce LLD DD, Professor of Assyriology at the University of Oxford, became so convinced of the accuracy of the Bible record that he wrote several books on the subject, including *Monument Facts and Higher Critical Fancies*.

All of the books by Professor Sayce in the British Library were destroyed in air raids during the Second World War. Five of his books are in the writer's possession, including the one mentioned above.

Where scholarship disagrees with the Bible, it is much wiser to reserve judgement and to believe the Bible, as it has so often been shown that doubts about the Bible text are simply the result of not knowing enough. So often have further discoveries confirmed the accuracy of the Bible, enough to convince men such as Professor Sayce, that it is only reasonable to believe that the Bible is true, and is the Word of God to us.

SHALMANESER III

The first Assyrian monarch we note is Shalmaneser III. In the Assyrian Transept is a Monolith of Shalmaneser. It tells how, on the occasion of one of his inroads into Syria, he found drawn up against him a strong allied army consisting of troops of Damascus, Hamath and others. Among the confederates were Ahab, king of Israel, and Ben-hadad, king of Syria. A battle which is described on the stone was fought at Qharquar, near Hamath on the Orontes.

Ashurnasirpal (c.883–859 B.C.)

Shalmaneser III (c.858–824 B.C.)

This battle is not mentioned in the Bible, nor was it conclusive, for despite his claims of an overwhelming victory, Shalmaneser, during his reign, made three further campaigns against the area without finally being victorious. It was in fact some 100 years later, in the reign of Tiglath-Pileser, that the last king of Damascus was on the throne, and Israel was finally carried away captive and the Northern Kingdom came to an end.

BEN-HADAD

The Bible records in 1 Kings 20 v 34 that **Ahab**, contrary to God's command (v 42), had spared the life of Ben-hadad and made a covenant with him.

There followed three years without war between Ahab and Ben-hadad (1 Kings 22 v 1) and it would appear that during that time the battle of Qharquar against Shalmaneser took place, for after three years we find Ahab in coalition with **Jehoshaphat**, king of Judah, moving once more against the king of Syria to recover Ramoth-Gilead which had been among the cities promised to him (1 Kings 20 v 34), but which had not been handed over. In this battle Ahab was slain (1 Kings 22 vv 29–36), as had been prophesied three years earlier: "Thus saith the Lord, Because thou hast let go out of thy hand a man whom I appointed to utter destruction, therefore thy life shall go for his life" (1 Kings 20 v 42).

The discovery of this monolith gave an incidental proof of the accuracy with which the cuneiform, or wedge-shaped, writing of the Assyrian monuments had been deciphered. The stone was found at Kurkh on the right bank of the Tigris, and when sent home was deciphered by Sir Henry Rawlinson. He read that Shalmaneser had set it up by the side of a similar inscription by his father Ashur-nasir-pal. Word was therefore sent to those who were exploring to dig again in the same place, and the companion monolith was found. The two monoliths now stand adjacent to one another in the Assyrian Transept.

THE MOABITE OR MESHA STONE

Ahab was succeeded by his son Ahaziah. In the Second Book of Kings, chapter 1, we read how Ahaziah died after a reign of only two years, and because he had no children, Jehoram, Ahab's second son, reigned in his stead.

Although not in this section of the Museum but in the Room of Writing, we now consider one of the most exciting and important exhibits concerning the Bible to be found in the Museum. This is the Moabite or Mesha Stone. This monolith erected by **King Mesha** in his city of Dibon in Moab, was discovered in 1868 and when deciphered confirmed and amplified the Biblical evidence about him.

The discovery of this stone created a veritable sensation because of its close connection with Old Testament history and excited widespread interest in Palestine excavations.

The story of its discovery is fascinating. It was found in 1868 by the CMS missionary, F A Klein, on the site of Dibon. The over-eager interest shown by Europeans caused the Arabs to destroy the stone by heating it over a fire and then dashing cold water over it, so causing it to split in pieces. The pieces were distributed among the tribes, but were gradually traced and bought and pieced together.

Rubbings and squeezings had been taken when it was found, so that the inscriptions could be read. With the help of these the fragments were put together and the stone now stands in the Louvre in Paris. The stone was offered to the Trustees of the Palestine Exploration Fund who turned the offer down. Thus the example in the Room of Writing is a replica of the original. The language of the stone differs only little from Biblical Hebrew.

One other point of great interest is that this stone bears "the earliest indubitable mention of the divine tetragrammaton outside the Bible" (*Bible and Spade*, Caiger). Reference will be made to the name Jehovah when the Ancient Manuscript Department is reached.

The Moabite Stone is brought in at this point because it fits in the chronological order of the kings of Israel.

In 2 Kings 3 vv 1–5 we read how **Jehoram** reigned over Israel. Verses 4 and 5 read thus: "And Mesha, king of Moab, was a sheepmaster, and rendered unto the king of Israel an hundred thousand lambs and an hundred thousand rams, with the wool. But it came to pass, when Ahab was dead, that the king of Moab rebelled against the king of Israel."

Mesha wrote: "I am Mesha, king of Moab, the Dibonite . . . **Omri**, king of Israel, humbled Moab many days . . . his son (Jehoram) succeeded him, and he also said, 'I will humble

51

Moabite on Mesha Stone: Louvre 5066

Carved Ivory Panel from Furniture
(see page 179)

Black Obelisk of
Shalmaneser

Photograph: BM

52

Moab.' In my days he spake this but I have triumphed over him and over his house . . ."

Following the revolt of Mesha, **Jehoram** and **Jehoshaphat**, king of Judah, joined forces to bring Mesha into subjection. From the Bible record it appears that in accordance with the prophecy of Elisha they had great success. When it seemed that final defeat was inevitable, Mesha sacrificed his eldest son as a burnt offering upon the city wall. The exact reason is not clear, but from that point Israel departed and returned to their own land (2 Kings 3 vv 26–27).

Mesha began to restore his sovereignty and finally expelled Israel from his land. He says, "I have triumphed but Israel has perished for ever."

THE BLACK OBELISK OF SHALMANESER

Returning to the objects in the Assyrian Transept, we easily discern the Black Obelisk of Shalmaneser. This monument was found by Layard in 1846 in the Imperial Palace at Nimrud. The rows of carving show conquered peoples from the empire bringing tribute to the king.

JEHU

On the second row is shown Jehu, king of Israel, or his envoy, offering his tribute and homage. A paper squeeze in the Museum states that Shalmaneser received tribute from Jehu during his expedition against Hazael (BM Guide A, page 30). As this event would have been within or very near his own territory it is very probable that the figure represented on the obelisk is Jehu himself.

Above this scene is written in Assyrian cuneiform, "The tribute of Jehu, son of Omri: I received from him silver, gold, a golden bowl, a golden vase with a pointed bottom, golden tumblers, golden buckets, tin, a staff for a king (and) Purukhti fruits" (*Illustrations of Old Testament History*, R D Barnett).

HAZAEL

This obelisk also mentions Hazael, king of Syria. Jehu and Hazael were the two whom Elijah was commanded to anoint (1 Kings 19 vv 15–18).

The Assyrians have recorded that Jehu was the son of Omri, when in fact he was a usurper, as was Hazael. This is understandable as Jehu succeeded the family of Ahab on the throne. Also Samaria itself was called Bit-Omri, The House of Omri.

SAMARIA

This agrees with the account of the founding of the city given in 1 Kings 16 vv 23–24: "In the thirty and first year of **Asa**, king of Judah, began **Omri** to reign over Israel, twelve years; six years he reigned in Tirzah. And he bought the hill Samaria of Shemer for two talents of silver, and he built on the hill, and called the name of the city which he built after the name of Shemer, owner of the hill, Samaria." More than just Samaria, the whole of the kingdom of Israel is called "The House of Omri" in Assyrian records, and its rulers sons of the House of Omri.

The historical text around the base of the obelisk describes the conquests of Shalmaneser. It states that he captured 1,121 chariots, 470 battle horses and the whole camp of Hazael, king of Damascus. It was at the time of this expedition that Jehu brought his tribute.

The Museum has the text of a squeeze taken from a fragment of the Annals of Shalmaneser regarding his campaign against Hazael. The text is as follows:

"In my eighteenth year for the sixteenth time I crossed the Euphrates. Hazael of Damascus trusted in the might of his army without number. He made Mount Shenir, the highest peak of the mountains which are as you come to Mount Lebanon, his fortress. I fought with him; I overthrew him; 16,000 of his fighting men I slew with weapons; 1,121 of his chariots, 470 of his horsemen, along with his camp, I took from him. To save his life he ascended (the country); I pursued after him. In Damascus his royal city, I shut him up; his plantations I cut down. To the mountains of the Hauran I went; cities innumerable I threw down, I dug up, I burned with fire, their spoil innumerable I carried away. To the mountains of Baal-rosh at the promontory of the sea I went; I made an image of my majesty there. At that time I received the tribute of the Tyrians, of the Sidonians and of Jehu, son of Omri" (*Assyria*, A H Sayce).

The rock carvings which Shalmaneser caused to be done in his honour may still be seen today. Shenir is Mount Hermon (see Deuteronomy 3 v 9).

Detail of Jehu offering tribute to Shalmaneser

Photograph: BM

Tiglath — Pileser III   *Photograph: BM*

TIGLATH-PILESER OR PUL

"In the days of **Pekah**, king of Israel, came Tiglath-Pileser, king of Assyria, and took Ijon, and Abel-beth-maachah, and Janoah, and Kedesh, and Hazor, and Gilead, and Galilee, all the land of Naphtali, and carried them captive to Assyria" (2 Kings 15 v 29).

In 2 Kings 15 v 19 it is recorded that a king of Assyria named Pul came against **Menahem**, king of Israel. However, no such king was known in the years 745–727 BC. During the reigns of Menahem, Pekahiah, Pekah, and into the reign of **Hoshea**, Tiglath-Pileser was king of Assyria. This would appear to be another Bible anomaly until it was discovered in Babylonian records that **Pul** was another name for Tiglath-Pileser. This was found recorded in the Babylonian Dynastic Tablets discovered by Dr Pinches. (See Dr Pinches, *The Old Testament in the Light of Historical Records*.)

Tiglath-Pileser built a new palace at **Nimrud**, and in the Nimrud Gallery is a sculptured slab from that palace showing the capture of a city in Gilead during the campaign mentioned in 2 Kings 15. There is also a slab in the Ancient Palestine Room showing an enemy horseman trying to ward off pursuers.

Dr R D Barnett describes the slab in the Nimrud Gallery thus:

"The city, standing on a mound, is surrounded by a double wall with towers, and has a citadel at one end. Assyrian officers are driving out booty in the form of fat-tailed rams, and Hebrew prisoners are carrying bundles, wearing West Semitic dress, turban with floppy top, fringed mantle and shirt, and boots with upward curving toes.

"In the central band is a passage from Tiglath-Pileser's historical annals, describing his campaigns in the North of Assyria.

"In the panel below is the king himself, standing in his state chariot beneath a parasol, and saluting some persons, perhaps officers with prisoners, who were probably depicted on an adjacent slab" (*Illustrations of Old Testament History*).

HOSHEA

In 2 Kings 17 we read that Hoshea reigned over Israel for nine years. Against him came up Shalmaneser king of Assyria, and Hoshea became his servant and gave him presents. However Hoshea rebelled against the king of Assyria, for he stopped paying tribute to Shalmaneser and sought help from So, king of Egypt (v 4). Shalmaneser then bound Hoshea in prison, went through all the land and besieged Samaria for three years.

SHALMANESER V AND SARGON

Shalmaneser V reigned for only five years and was succeeded by Sargon. From the end of verse 4 of 2 Kings 17, the king of Assyria is not identified by name; so that verse 5 would read the king of Assyria (Shalmaneser) and verse 6 the king of Assyria (Sargon).

Sargon was a general in Shalmaneser's army and on usurping the throne he assumed the venerable title of Sargon. His name was unknown apart from the mention in Isaiah 20 v 1, until the advent of Biblical archaeology. In 1843 P E Botta, the French Consular Agent at Mosul, discovered Sargon's palace at Khorsabad, and now Sargon is one of the best known of the Assyrian emperors (*Archaeology and the Old Testament*, Unger).

On the Nimrud Prism, Sargon claims to have captured Samaria and to have deported Israel to cities of Assyria. Sargon lists the fall of Samaria as the outstanding event of the first year of his reign: "At the beginning of my rule, in my first year of reign . . . (the people of Samaria) 27,290 . . . I carried away" (Unger). This is a significant example of the vindication of the Bible record by further discovery.

JAREB

It is thought by many that while Sargon took the name of one of the earliest Assyrian kings when he usurped the throne, his name before then was Jareb, and that the two passages in Hosea refer to him. Hosea 5 v 13 says that Ephraim and Judah went to the Assyrian and sent to king Jareb: "yet could he not heal you, nor cure you of your wound." Hosea 10 vv 5–7 tells how Samaria should be carried to Assyria for a present to king Jareb.

In the Museum is a fragment of a small cylinder of Shalmaneser V, who besieged Samaria. It records his

Sargon II   Photograph: BM

Colossal winged bull from Sargon's Palace at Khorsabad

restoration of a temple in Babylonia after it had been damaged by flood (Unger).

From Sargon's palace at **Khorsabad** come two colossal winged bulls standing at the Khorsabad Entrance. These were from a gateway into the citadel, and represented guardian figures. Each weighs some 16 tons (BM Guide 1976).

Sargon built a new capital at Khorsabad, and "in the Khorsabad Entrance is a relief from the palace there showing the king receiving a state official, possibly the Turtanu or Commander-in-Chief" (*Illustrations of Old Testament History*, R D Barnett).

One of the cities to which the Israelites of Samaria were deported was **Habor** (2 Kings 17 v 6). In the Syrian Room are some sculptures from the wall of a palace there.

In the Assyrian Room is another pair of colossal winged figures. These have the bodies of a lion, the head of a man and the wings of an eagle. They stood at one end of Ashurnasirpal's throne room, facing the throne and guarding the way up into the roof. On closer examination it will be seen that each of these figures, as with the colossal bulls, has five legs, giving the appearance of four legs when viewed from different angles.

Here too are reproductions of Assyrian doors from a small town near Nimrud called Balawat. The full scale model against the wall dates from the reign of Shalmaneser of Ahab and Jehu's time. The metal strips are electrotype reproductions of the original bronzes, which are in the showcase to the left. "The pictures, many of which have cuneiform captions, exemplify the range of the subject matter of Assyrian narrative art. Battles, sieges, captives, tribute-bearers and occasionally a more elaborate event, are represented in the minutest detail; little is left to the spectator's imagination" (R D Barnett).

THE LACHISH ROOM

"The Assyrian came down like a wolf on the fold, and his cohorts were gleaming in purple and gold." In the ante-room are sculptures and inscriptions of Tiglath-Pileser, and in the farthest corner, the noted wall picture depicting Sennacherib before Lachish (2 Chronicles 32 v 9): "After this did Sennacherib send his servants to Jerusalem (but he himself laid siege against Lachish, and all his power with him)."

The inscription in front of the king says: "Sennacherib, king of hosts, king of Assyria, sat upon his throne of state, and the spoil of the city of Lachish passed before him."

The Bible account of this campaign against Hezekiah, king of Judah, is given in 2 Chronicles 32 vv 1–23 and Isaiah 36 and 37. In the account given in 2 Kings 18 and 19, we read that Hezekiah paid tribute to Sennacherib; this tribute is referred to on the Taylor Prism, which will be spoken of later.

SENNACHERIB

When Sargon was killed in battle, his son Sennacherib succeeded him. Sennacherib moved his capital to Nineveh and built a new palace there. This palace was decorated with some two miles of sculptured slabs.

The wall sculpture of Sennacherib before Lachish is described in the British Museum Guide 1976 thus: "On the left we see the Assyrian army 'like the wolf on the fold', advancing to the attack through mountainous country. There are Assyrian troops in pointed helmets and a host of imperial levies, including some from Southern Iran. As they approach the city, the slingers and archers open fire; the city itself is represented at a later point in the contest. Steep ramps have been built against the walls, and Assyrian forces charge up them, headed by siege engines. The defenders throw missiles of every kind, but cannot prevent the outworks falling: captives are already being led out of the gate.

"Further to the right the captives are brought before Sennacherib. Some have their possessions with them, piled in carts ready for the journey into exile; others have been condemned to death. The king watches proceedings from a sumptuous throne set up outside his tent; his bodyguard and chariot wait behind him."

ASSYRIAN PRACTICES

"The barbarities which followed the capture of a town would be almost incredible, were they not a subject of boast in the inscriptions which record them. Ashurnasirpal's cruelties were especially revolting. Pyramids of human heads marked the path of the conqueror; boys and girls were burned alive, or reserved for a worse fate; men were impaled, flayed alive, blinded or deprived of their hands and feet, of their ears and noses; while the women and the children were carried into slavery, the captured city plundered and reduced to ashes, and

Sennacherib before Lachish

61

the trees in the neighbourhood cut down" (*Assyria: Its Princes, Priests and People*, A H Sayce).

In contrast with the Assyrian practice of destroying all the trees, instructions to the Children of Israel were very specific: they were not to cut down any fruit trees when besieging a city, and only other trees as were necessary for use in the siege. The denuding of land of trees which occurred during the four hundred years of Turkish rule of Palestine was one of the major factors in turning the area into one of the seven deserts of the world (see Deuteronomy 20 vv 19–20).

HEZEKIAH

Hezekiah, king of Judah, together with some of the neighbouring kings, rebelled against Sennacherib and refused to pay tribute. The Ethiopian king of Egypt promised to support them against the Assyrians. Padi, the king of Ekron, who remained faithful to the Assyrians, was carried in chains to Jerusalem.

To punish the rebel kings and to restore his sovereignty, Sennacherib moved against the West, and finally attacked the kingdom of Judah. The story is told in 2 Kings 18 vv 13–19 and v 37. Sennacherib's version is recorded on the "Taylor Prism" which is in the Room of Writing. It is generally agreed that the inscription of Sennacherib, though differing from the Biblical account in some particulars, really confirms it at virtually every point.

In 2 Kings 18 vv 13–16 we read how the king of Assyria came up against all the fenced cities of Judah and took them. Hezekiah became afraid and sent to the king, who was besieging Lachish, to the south-west of Jerusalem, saying, "I have offended; return from me: that which thou puttest on me will I bear." Sennacherib laid a tribute on Hezekiah, which Hezekiah raised by taking all the silver in the house of the Lord, the silver from his own house and gold from the temple, and sent it to Sennacherib.

The king of Assyria's response was to send three officials with a great host against Jerusalem. Tartan, Rabsaris and Rabshakeh were for long thought to be the names of the three men, but now it is known that they were titles: Tartan, Commander-in-Chief; Rabshakeh, Chief Officer or Vizier; and Rabsaris, Chief Eunuch.

Rabshakeh urged the Jews to surrender and be taken peaceably into exile. He also warned them against relying on Egypt (verse 21). This warning proved correct, for in the meantime a huge host of Egyptians and Ethiopians were routed by Sennacherib.

Messages were again sent to Jerusalem that it was no use trusting in God to deliver them, for, "Behold, thou hast heard what the kings of Assyria have done to all the lands, by destroying them utterly: and shalt thou be delivered?" In 2 Kings 19 vv 35–37 we read how God did deliver Jerusalem and what happened to Sennacherib: "And it came to pass that night, that the angel of the Lord went out, and smote in the camp of the Assyrians an hundred four score and five thousand (185,000): and when they arose early in the morning, behold, they were all dead corpses. So Sennacherib, king of Assyria, departed and went and returned, and dwelt at Nineveh. And it came to pass, as he was worshipping in the house of Nisroch his god, that Adrammelech and Sharezer his sons smote him with the sword: and they escaped into the land of Armenia. And **Esarhaddon** his son reigned in his stead."

This is wonderfully confirmed by the Assyrian records. Sennacherib did return to Nineveh and never again invaded the West. He was murdered by two of his sons.

These two brothers fled to an insurgent king of Armenia. About eight weeks after the murder of the old king, a battle was fought in Cappadocia between Esarhaddon and the forces under the brothers and the Armenians. Esarhaddon was completely victorious and was proclaimed king.

On the Taylor Prism, Sennacherib makes some claims which it would seem were never realised. Also there appears to be a discrepancy in the king's recorded amount of silver paid by Hezekiah and the Bible account. Professor Sayce says of this, "There is, however, no exaggeration in the amount of silver Sennacherib claims to have received, since 800 talents of silver are equivalent to the 300 talents stated in the Bible to have been given, when reckoned according to the standard of values in use at the time in Nineveh." Today we should call it the rate of exchange.

In the account of his campaign Sennacherib of course says nothing about the disaster which befell his army in front of Jerusalem, and which obliged him to return ignominiously to Assyria without attempting to capture the city, and to deal with it and Hezekiah as was his custom to deal with rebellious kings, which he certainly would have done had he captured Jerusalem, for he was "a fiendishly cruel and inhuman ruler, guilty of impaling and flaying his foes alive and other incredible atrocities" (*Archaeology and the Old Testament*, Unger). On the Taylor Prism Sennacherib records, "I shut up Hezekiah like a bird in a cage," but no more.

ESARHADDON

A clay tablet, now in the Room of Writing, contains a letter from Sennacherib to his son Esarhaddon. This tablet is known as the "Will of Sennacherib" as it refers to certain objects given by him to Esarhaddon.

In the first year of his reign Esarhaddon rebuilt Babylon, giving it back its captured deities, its plunder, and its people. Henceforth Babylon became the second capital of the empire, the court residing alternately there and at Nineveh. It was while Esarhaddon was holding his winter court at Babylon, that king Manasseh of Judah was brought to him as a prisoner (2 Chronichles 33 v 11).

The principal achievement of Esarhaddon's reign was his conquest of the ancient monarchy of Egypt. In 675 BC the Assyrian army started for the banks of the Nile. Four years later Memphis was taken on the 22nd of Tamuz or June, and **Tirhakah**, the Egyptian king, compelled to fly first to Thebes and then into Ethiopia. Egypt was divided into twenty satrapies, governed partly by Assyrians and partly by native princes.

On his return to Assyria, Esarhaddon associated Ashurbanipal, the eldest of his four sons, in the government on the 12th April 669 BC. He died two years later on the 12th October, when again on his way to Egypt.

Esarhaddon is undoubtedly the "cruel and fierce king" of Isaiah 19 v 4. In verses 1–10 this chapter foretells the fall of Egypt. This was accomplished by Esarhaddon who "realised the highest ambition of all Assyrians — the conquest of Egypt" (*Archaeology and the Old Testament*, Unger).

A notable part of the prophecy fulfilled in modern times is in verse 7 of Isaiah 19: "The paper reeds by the brooks, by the mouth of the brooks, and everything sown by the brooks shall wither, be driven away and be no more." In the book *Egypt, The Black Land* by Paul Jordan (Phaidon, Oxford 1976), we are told that papyrus reed is only now found in the far southern reaches of the Nile, so no longer in the Nile delta at the mouth of the brooks and all over the watered part of Egypt as in ancient times.

"Esarhaddon's brilliant victory over the Egyptian king was celebrated with a victory stela set up at Senjirli in North Syria, and discovered in 1888 by a German expedition. In Ezra 4 v 2 Esarhaddon is mentioned as the king who colonised Samaria" (Unger).

MANASSEH

In 2 Chronicles 33 vv 1–20 is the record of Manasseh as being amongst the kings summoned to Nineveh to receive orders upon the rebuilding of the palace there. There is no known Assyrian record of Manasseh's Babylonian captivity but the inscriptions prove that Esarhaddon did in fact rebuild Babylon on a grand scale.

ASHURBANIPAL (669–633 BC)

We now turn our attention to the last "great" king of Assyria, the grandson of Sennacherib, Ashurbanipal. The Assyrian empire was at its height; it would seem incredible that within twenty years of the death of Ashurbanipal Nineveh would be destroyed and, as the prophet Nahum had foretold, "its bars devoured by fire" (Nahum 3 v 7 and v 13). Evidence of this may be seen on the wall sculptures from Nineveh, some still blackened by fire. In the past attempts have been made to clean them, but the evidence of the certainty of God's judgement remains.

Ashurbanipal is only once referred to in the Bible (in Ezra 4 v 10), and then as "the great and noble Asnapper (who) brought over and set in the cities of Samaria" peoples from various conquered nations, whilst Israel was carried away into Assyria. (See 2 Kings 17 v 6.)

Professor Sayce describes Ashurbanipal as "luxurious, ambitious and cruel, but a munificent patron of literature. The libraries of Babylon were ransacked for ancient texts, and scribes kept busily employed at Nineveh inscribing new editions of older works." It was from this source that many of the 30,000 cuneiform tablets in the Museum came. From this great library of Ashurbanipal came the Babylonian account of

Ashurbanipal hunting from his chariot as attendants ward off lions with spears

Onegars (wild asses) fleeing from the hunt. A mare looks back helplessly as her colt is overtaken by the dogs

the Fall of man, and of the Flood; also confirmation of 2 Kings 19 vv 36–37, where we are told of Sennacherib's return to Nineveh after the debacle outside the walls of Jerusalem as recorded in v 35 of that chapter, and of his murder by two of his sons, who then fled to Armenia.

"Unlike his father, Ashurbanipal refused to face hardships of campaign. His armies were led by generals who were required to send dispatches from time to time to the king. It was evident that a purely military empire, like that of Assyria, could not last long, when its ruler had ceased to take an active part in military affairs. At first the veterans of Esarhaddon even extended the empire of Ashurbanipal; but before his death the empire was shattered irretrievably. It is characteristic of Ashurbanipal that his lion hunts were mere battues (shoots) in which tame animals were released from cages and lashed to make them run; in contrast to lion hunts in the open field in which his war-like predecessors had delighted" (Professor Sayce, *Assyria: Its Princes, Priests and People*).

In the Assyrian Saloon and Basement are wall sculptures from the palace of Ashurbanipal at Nineveh; these were discovered by H Rassam in 1853. These sculptures have been described by Professor Sayce as the best of Assyrian works for freedom and skill, with the landscape either left bare or indicated in outline, thus focusing the attention on the principal sculpture.

HUNTING

After his defeat of the king of Babylon in 649 BC, Ashurbanipal constructed a new palace at Nineveh which he adorned with a series of magnificent stone reliefs illustrating his campaigns and scenes from the Royal Hunt.

We see illustrated on the reliefs, catching deer in a net, shooting gazelle from a pit (in the same way that game is driven towards the guns nowadays), hunting the wild ass and slaying lions. In amongst the fleeing onagers, pursued by dogs, may be seen a mare looking back helplessly at her foal who is about to be overtaken.

In the sculpture illustrating the lion hunt we see spectators who have stationed themselves in a place of safety on a mound, and the king himself shooting lions from his chariot. We see lions being released from a cage and lions being driven by huntsmen. In one scene lions are being fought on foot.

Surely none but the most indifferent can fail to be moved within whilst looking upon these scenes from Old Testament times from the palace of Ashurbanipal at the Assyrian Royal City of Nineveh, after lying hidden in the ground for some 2,000 years. Perhaps we are reminded of Rudyard Kipling's words, "Lo, all our pomp of yesterday, is one with Nineveh and Tyre. Judge of the nations spare us yet, lest we forget — lest we forget."

Within a few years of the destruction of Nineveh the remnants of the once mighty Assyrian empire had disappeared. The Babylonians led by the Chaldean prince Nabopolassar struck again for independence. Nabopolassar defeated the Assyrians outside Babylon and took the throne. He had founded the Neo-Babylonian empire. The Babylonians and the Medes besieged Nineveh and broke through the defences, destroying it utterly. Three years after the fall of Nineveh the mighty empire had crumbled and ceased to exist. "Her place on the international scene was taken by the new Babylonian empire which, in turn, inaugurated a new historical epoch full of significance for Israel" (*Pictorial Biblical Encyclopedia*, Cornfeld).

Note

* Regarding Professor Sayce's identification of Amraphel of Genesis 14 with Hammurabi the law giver: the question has been raised as there was more than one king of that name.

This is not really important; the fact is that, as Professor Sayce states, the name Amraphel is letter for letter the name Hammurabi. The etymological identification is not in doubt, proving that Amraphel was not an invented name, as critics have said, but a real king.

View of Sculpture Gallery with the Rosetta Stone on left

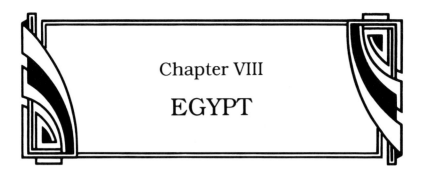

Chapter VIII

EGYPT

Passing through the doors of the Great Russell Street entrance to the Museum into the Entrance Hall, we turn left into the Card and Publication Gallery, on towards the restaurant and turn right across the Assyrian Transept into the Egyptian Sculpture Gallery.

THE PHARAOHS

"The Egyptian Galleries are full of the remains from the land of the Pharaohs. The eyes of Jacob and his sons may have looked many times on some of these earlier statues, and Moses and Aaron would probably have seen still more of them.

"There were many Pharaohs connected with Bible history, but it is not possible to identify every one of them by their Egyptian names.

"First there was the Pharaoh of Genesis 12, whose court Abraham and Sarah visited.

"Then there was the Pharaoh of the story of Joseph. This Pharaoh was of the Hyksos or Shepherd Kings" (Mrs Habershon). Later we shall see items connected with these kings.

AMOSIS I

"Now there arose up a new king over Egypt, which knew not Joseph" (Exodus 1 v 8). This would have been the first king of a new dynasty who conquered the Hyksos* and drove them out of Egypt, pursuing them back into Palestine from whence they originated. They would have been kindly disposed to Jacob and his sons, a pastoral people from the area whence they themselves came. It is significant to note in passing that the

*See footnote on page 105

King List of Rameses II has no mention of the Hyksos rulers in it.

By the time that the "new king" arose, the Children of Israel had so increased that they outnumbered the Egyptians (Exodus 1 vv 8–9). This so greatly concerned the Egyptians that they oppressed the Children of Israel and set over them taskmasters.

In verse 5 of Exodus 2 we meet the **daughter of Pharaoh** who adopted Moses. Then the Pharaoh of verse 23 of the same chapter, of whom it is said, "In process of time, the king of Egypt died." On to verse 25, "And God looked upon the children of Israel, and God had respect unto them"; so Moses is brought into the picture and also the Pharaoh on whom fell the Plagues of Egypt.

Next is the "firstborn" who was slain by the destroying angel. For many years after the Exodus of the Children of Israel there is silence in the Scripture about Egypt.

In 1 Kings 3 v 1 it is recorded that Solomon married Pharaoh's daughter and brought her into the city of David.

1 Kings 11 v 40 tells that Jeroboam fled to **Shishak**, king of Egypt. Again in 1 Kings 14 vv 25–26 we read Shishak came against Jerusalem and took away the treasures of the Lord's house, also the shields of gold which Solomon had made. King Rehoboam replaced these with shields of brass. In 2 Chronicles 12 vv 1–12 there is an extended account of this event.

Our next Pharaoh is **So**, king of Egypt, with whom Hoshea, king of Israel, sought an alliance against Shalmaneser of Assyria to whom he was a tributary.

Hezekiah, king of Judah, formed an alliance with **Tirhakah** the king of Ethiopia and Egypt. His name is mentioned in Isaiah 37 v 9.

There was much truth in part of Sennacherib's message to Hezekiah, "Lo, thou trustest in the staff of this broken reed, on Egypt; whereon if a man lean it will go into his hand and pierce it; so is Pharaoh king of Egypt to all that trust in him" (Isaiah 36 v 6), for so it proved throughout the history of Israel.

In 2 Kings 23 v 29–35, the name of **Pharaoh-Necho** is recorded four times in connection with the kings of Judah, Josiah, Jehoahaz and Jehoiakim.

Necho and his allies accomplished the overthrow of the Assyrians in 609 BC but four years later was himself defeated by Nebuchadnezzar, king of Babylon.

In Jeremiah 46 we read the prophecy of Jeremiah against Egypt and the army of Pharaoh-Necho.

Hophra, the successor of Pharaoh-Necho, induced Zedekiah to break his allegiance to Babylon. He is the Pharaoh of Jeremiah 47 v 1, who "smote Gaza". Hophra is also the Pharaoh of Jeremiah 37 vv 5–8 whose "army came forth out of Egypt," which caused the Chaldeans to raise the siege of Jerusalem for a time, but they returned and captured Zedekiah and the city. The eyes of Zedekiah were put out and he was carried in chains to Babylon, where he was in prison until he died, in accordance with the prophecy of Ezekiel 17 vv 16–17: "As I live, saith the Lord God, surely in the place where the king (Nebuchadnezzar) dwelleth that made him (Zedekiah) king, whose oath he despised and whose covenant he brake, even with him (Nebuchadnezzar) in the midst of Babylon, he (Zedekiah) shall die. Neither shall Pharaoh (Hophra) with his mighty army and great company make for him in the war . . ."

The fulfilment of this prophecy is recorded in Jeremiah 52 vv 10–11: "And the king of Babylon slew the sons of Zedekiah before his eyes: he slew also all the princes of Judah in Riblah. Then he put out the eyes of Zedekiah; and the king of Babylon bound him in chains, and carried him to Babylon, and put him in prison till the day of his death."

Later the Babylonians returned and completed the destruction of Jerusalem and carried away the remaining treasures of the Lord's house. The temple of Solomon was razed and the walls of the city broken down. The temple lay in ruins until the days of **Cyrus**, king of Persia, as may be read in the Book of Ezra and in 2 Chronicles 36 vv 22–23.

A few years later Nebuchadnezzar invaded Egypt, slew Hophra, set up another king and carried those that were left of the Jewish people who had fled there, captive to Babylon. (See Josephus, Antiquities Book 10, chapter 9, paragraph 7.)

Thus from the beginning of Israel's history and throughout the centuries, they were constantly involved with Egypt.

It is interesting to read of these links as we stand in the presence of the colossal heads and sculptures of the Pharaohs in the Egyptian Galleries of the British Museum.

In Bay No 69 is a limestone stela of the Pharaoh Hophra of Jeremiah 47, No EA 1358 (Wahibre or Apries). The stela depicts the king offering to deities. Hophra was overthrown by Amosis, one of his generals, in about 580 BC.

There are two factors worthy of note before we move around the galleries. One is that in Assyria a predecessor's monuments and inscriptions were treated with great reverence. Many inscriptions ended with a curse on those who should in any way damage them, and invoked blessing on those who should preserve them.

In contrast, the Pharaohs thought nothing of erasing the names of their predecessors, and of carving their own names instead. Rameses II is particularly well known for doing this.

The second point to note is that the early chronology of Egypt is open to question. The British Museum Guide C, p222, has this to say on the subject: "Not only is the order of succession of the kings of these (earliest) dynasties unknown, but authorities differ greatly in their estimate of the length of the period of their rule."

At the entrance to the Southern Sculpture Gallery are two seated statues of the Pharaoh **Amenophis III** (Amenhotep), Nos E A 1 and 2. Amenophis III was one of the Pharaohs to whom the Tell-el-Amarna tablets were addressed. We shall see some of these tablets later in the Room of Writing. It was on the evidence of these tablets that Col C R Conder named Thutmose III as the Pharaoh of the oppression.

THE ROSETTA STONE

Passing between the statues, immediately to the left is one of the Museum's greatest treasures, the Rosetta Stone. The story of how this stone was acquired may be worth telling here.

On the 19th May 1798 a French fleet of almost 200 ships set sail from Toulon under sealed orders, a vast latter-day Armada of over 14,000 men, plus animals, guns and munitions. The flagship was the 120-gun triple-decker, L'Orient. On board, with the Admiral of the Fleet, was Napoleon Bonaparte.

Their objective was Egypt; they aimed to "rescue" Egypt from its Mameluke rulers and to add the country to the French empire.

As well as the warlike cargo, the ships carried 167 scientists and technicians with many eminent scholars. The 16 cartographers and surveyors were to play a very important part in the birth of Egyptology.

On the way to Egypt the French captured Malta and took on board L'Orient the treasure of the Knights, valued at some 7,000,000 gold francs.

Taharqua and Ram (see page 87)

Photograph: BM

The Rosetta Stone

On the first of July 1798 disembarkation began near Alexandria. The assault began early on the 2nd July, and after only one day the city surrendered to Napoleon.

After a week or so the army set off towards Cairo and the Pyramids. The battle for Cairo lasted about two hours, with terrible carnage amongst the Mamelukes. Two days later Napoleon entered Cairo.

Whilst Napoleon was safely installed in his HQ in Cairo things were happening elsewhere. In the Mediterranean, Nelson and the British fleet were looking for the French. Nelson was aware that the French fleet had left Toulon, and had made an informed guess as to their destination, finally learning that the French had sailed for Alexandria.

The British followed suit and at length sighted the French at anchor in Aboukir Bay, about 8 miles west of Alexandria. When the French were sighted Nelson ordered dinner and the attack in that order. With his captains he had already worked out various battle plans, remarking that the outcome of the battle would see him either in the House of Lords or Westminster Abbey.

Aboukir Bay is a magnificent long curve of shallow, shelving beach. No reliable charts of it existed, so the French admiral had anchored his men o'war in line about 1½ miles off shore with some 50 yards between them. Reasoning that their land-ward side was protected by the shallowness of the water, most of the fleet had withdrawn their land-ward guns.

In the early afternoon of 1st August working parties were ashore foraging, digging wells or fetching provisions from Alexandria and Rosetta, when the British fleet appeared. In accordance with their prearranged plan, the British sailed straight for the French line, helped along by the late afternoon north breeze, and passed between the westernmost of the French ships and the shore, missing the shoals and coming along their land-ward side, broadsiding as they went. The captain's thirteen year old midshipman son, on the French flagship, achieved immortality among the heroes that night, dying with his father when the ship blew up, sending the treasure of the Knights of Malta hurtling into the night sky above the bay. It was of him that Dorothea Hemans wrote the poem:

"The boy stood on the burning deck,
Whence all but he had fled."

There is another account of the incident which does not tie up with that.

Before the battle was over, Nelson had written a dispatch to George II, which began, "Almighty God has blessed His Majesty's arms . . ." Only four of the French ships escaped. On the morning of 1st August the French had been masters of Egypt. In one day the navy had thrown away the army's gains and lost the Empire. Napoleon and the French were cut off in Egypt. Despite the English blockade of the Egyptian coast, Napoleon with a few others managed to escape, abandoning the army to its fate.

In the early spring of 1801 a British combined naval and military force arrived off Alexandria. The British army commanded by Sir Ralph Abercrombie landed on 8th March. The French were defeated at the Battle of Alexandria on 21st March 1801.

Under the Treaty of Alexandria, Article 16, the French had to hand over all antiquities found by them. An inventory of fifteen antiquities in the possession of the French was found amongst the papers of Col Sir Tomkyns Hilgrove Turner and is now in the Manuscript Department of the British Library (BL ADD Ms 46839F).

The chief prize was item No 8 — the Rosetta Stone, a piece of inscribed basalt rock, found during the strengthening of fortifications by an officer of Napoleon's Engineers, Lt P F X Bouchard, at Fort Julien on the Rosetta mouth of the Nile in 1799. He recognised its possible importance and reported it to General Menou, who promptly claimed it for himself. Eventually it was collected from his house by a detachment of artillerymen. In the year 1802 it was deposited in the British Museum. The Rosetta Stone held the key to the future of Egyptology.

The Rosetta Stone is inscribed in three scripts and two languages, Hieroglyphic, Demotic and Greek — Hieroglyphic, the ancient picture language of Egypt; Demotic, a cursive script used generally. The Greek could be read, and revealed that the stone contained a decree conferring honours on **Ptolemy V** for the favours shown to priests and temples.

It was an English physician and physicist, Dr Thomas Young, who came to the conclusion that the Hieroglyphic was a mixture of alphabetic and phonetic signs.

Amosis I: the first King
of the 18th Dynasty —
the only figure known
to have survived
(see page 70)

Green Schist Head:
Thutmose III or Hatshepsut
Co-Regent   Photograph: BM

In the Hieroglyphic part were certain words enclosed in a cartouche. It was assumed that such words would be proper names. By comparison with the Bankes Obelisk at Kingston Lacy in Dorset the names of Ptolemy and **Cleopatra** were deciphered.

The conclusion of **Dr Young** was basic to the decipherment of the Hieroglyphics, but the one to whom most credit goes in the work is Champollion. By the time of his death in 1832, **Champollion**, the brilliant French scholar, had deciphered correctly the names and titles of all the Roman emperors, as they appeared in Hieroglyphic, made a classified list of the signs, and formulated a system of grammar.

On the wall immediately behind the Rosetta Stone is a display illustrating the development of the Hieroglyphic, Hieratic and Demotic scripts.

Upon the wall opposite is the **King List of Rameses II**. This gives another example of the tendency of Rameses to re-write history to suit himself as he makes no mention in the list of the **Hyksos** rulers of the 13th to 17th Dynasties.

The red granite lions behind the two seated figures are also attributable to Amenophis III, the one on the right being inscribed later by Tutankhamen and later still by a ruler named Amanislo.

Beyond this introductory area, the gallery is arranged in chronological order beginning with the Old Kingdom and ending at the northern end with the Graeco-Roman period, thus covering a period of about 3,000 years, up to 440 AD. The southern end of the Southern Side Gallery has exhibits from even earlier, from about 3,100 BC to about 2,686 BC.

To the south of the steps leading to the Southern Side Gallery is the seated statue in red granite of **Sobkemsaf I**, a king of the Hyksos period, about 1630 BC (E A 871).

Entering the side gallery by these steps and looking to the left, a Thutmoside head in green schist can be seen. This is of particular interest to us as it represents either Thutmose III or his sister and co-regent, **Queen Hatshepsut** (E A 986).

The question immediately springs to mind, "Could this queen, in her earlier years, have been the 'daughter of Pharaoh' who drew the infant Moses out of the water?"

In the Museum, **Thutmose** is named as Tuthmosis, but Unger retains the older spelling. This is of special interest as showing that Moses had the name of Pharaoh. Mose, pronounced in Hebrew Moshe, is in English Moses.

It would seem that the prospect before Moses was the throne itself, being brought up as the son of the co-ruler. This adds weight and point to the verses in Hebrews which say of Moses, "By faith Moses when he was come to years, refused to be called the son of Pharaoh's daughter; choosing rather to suffer affliction with the people of God, than to enjoy the pleasures of sin for a season; esteeming the reproach of Christ greater riches than the treasures of Egypt" (Hebrews 11 vv 24–26a). The phrase "treasures of Egypt" is significant, for none other than Pharaoh could lay claim to all. After the period of Joseph, all ultimately belonged to the Pharaoh. Estates could not be left to individuals but only to families who held them under Pharaoh.

This fact is a remarkable example of a hidden confirmation of the Bible story of Joseph, where we are told that in exchange for food Joseph acquired all the land of Egypt for Pharaoh. It could be that this head in the middle of the southern end of the side gallery, is one of the most exciting pieces in the Museum for us.

THUTMOSE III

Most of the pieces shown in this area are of the period of Thutmose III. No EA 888 bears the cartouche of Thutmose on its right shoulder. Two of the other statues are of **Senenmut**, the architect of Queen Hatshepsut's great temple at Deir-el-Bahri. No 1513 shows him as a squatting figure and No 174 represents him seated on a throne holding in his lap his ward, Queen Hatshepsut's daughter, the **Princess Neferure**. The paintings on the walls of this section are also of the 18th Dynastic period. One of the figures here is a finely worked figure of Amosis I, the founder of the 18th Dynasty, and probably the "king who knew not Joseph" (No EA 3219).

Returning to the main gallery we confront the colossal head and arm of red granite. For many years this was designated as of Thutmose III; today, however, it is suggested that it may be representative of Amenophis III. To quote from *Egyptian Sculpture* by T G H James and W V Davies (BM Pub 1983), "The statue is now however thought on good stylistic grounds to belong to Amenophis III, though it has been suggested that some modification may have been made to it in the Rameside

Standing Figure of Thutmose III
(see page 83)

Colossal Head   Thutmose III

period." In other words, to alter it from the style of a Thutmoside ruler to that of a Rameside one. As has already been noted, "the usurpation of earlier rulers was a common practice of the Rameside kings" — perhaps not very positive ground for such an alteration in opinion.

This head and arm was discovered by Belzoni at Karnak in 1817. The torso had been found lying in situ in the precincts of the temple of Mut. The head weighs 6 tons; if complete with the body it would be much too tall to stand in the gallery.

THE PHARAOH OF THE OPPRESSION

This brings us to the question, "Who was the Pharaoh of the oppression?"

To seek to answer this question we leave the Egyptologists, who mostly favour **Rameses II**, and turn to the Bible. In 1 Kings 6 v 1 is given a very clear indication of the date of the Exodus and thus also of the Pharaoh of the oppression. It is significant that according to this verse the Exodus would have been about 1450 BC, probably a few years later than the exact year in which the reign of Thutmose III ended.

Professor Garstang who excavated Jericho for six years in the 1930s dated the conquest to exactly this period. He says that if the date of the Exodus had not been brought into question by the rise of modern criticism in the nineteenth century, then his findings at Jericho would not have been questioned.

Garstang found **Joshua's Jericho** exactly as one would expect from the Bible record, even to a part of the wall still standing with a house upon it. No ordinary burning took place here; great heaps of ash and charcoal five feet deep were found piled in the streets, and the walls fallen down exactly as described in the Bible so that every man went up into the city "straight before him".

Dame Kathleen Kenyon denied all this, filled in Garstang's excavations with debris from her own and declared that there was no city there at all when the Israelites arrived. It is recorded that her expedition found only "a floor, a hearth and one pot" as evidence of occupation at that time (*Walls of Jericho*).

This is a serious matter, for if Rameses II was the Pharaoh of the oppression, then the Bible is quite wrong. Here the supporters of Rameses II must encounter difficulty, for it is generally recognised that far from relying on oral tradition, as had for so long been supposed, the ancient historians were copying from written records, even in the case of Moses, the Creation and the Flood.

This being so, if the building of Solomon's temple was recorded at that period there would only be some 200 years between that event and the Exodus, if Rameses II were the Pharaoh of the oppression. To us thinking back, this would have been around the beginning of the 19th century. Such a mistake would have been so obvious to the writers that it would never have been recorded.

The relevant verse is **1 Kings 6 v 1**: "And it came to pass in the four hundred and eightieth year after the children of Israel were come out of the land of Egypt, in the fourth year of Solomon's reign over Israel, in the month of Zif, which is the second month, that he began to build the house of the Lord" — surely an explicit and detailed statement not to be lightly passed over.

Another Biblical confirmation of the date of the Exodus is to be found in the New Testament at **Acts 13 v 20**, where Paul says that God gave them judges for about four hundred and fifty years until Samuel the prophet, when the Israelites desired a king and God gave them Saul. Saul became king, according to the generally accepted dating, in about 1060 BC, which confirms the period of c 1400 BC as the date of the Exodus (note the wording of the passage quoted: "about").

John C Whitcomb Jr, Th D, Professor of Old Testament at Grace Theological Seminary, USA, gives the date of Samuel at Bethel as 1067 BC, and Saul some years later than 1060 BC, but this does not alter the naming of Thutmose III as the Pharaoh of the oppression.

As has already been said, the earlier Bible scholars such as Col Conder had no doubt as to the accuracy of the Bible record, which has been confirmed by archaeology in so many instances. We, too, can be certain that the Bible is true and that **Thutmose III** was the Pharaoh of the oppression.

One of the main planks of the modern theory is that the Bible says that the Children of Israel built "treasure cities Pithom and Raamses". This is not a strong argument on which to base such a conclusion as one may discover from reading Professor John Bimson's book *Redating the Exodus and Conquest* (Almond Press, Sheffield). It is not absolutely certain that the Raamses of Exodus and Rameses refer to the same name.

To continue our tour of the galleries, to the left of the colossal head and arm is a red granite standing figure of possibly Thutmose III, again with the name of Rameses II and also Merneptah inscribed upon it. (Regarding the name Thutmose, it is interesting to note that David Kossof in his book of Bible stories mentions that Moses is much more Egyptian than Hebrew, as has already been referred to.) The number of this figure is EA 61.

THE GODS OF EGYPT

Further on the left, standing with backs to the wall, are four black granite figures of Sakhmut, the fierce leonine goddess, all with heads of a lioness. These are ascribed to Amenophis III (Nos EA 76, 57, 62 and 80).

As we move around the Egyptian Galleries we see many representations of the gods of Egypt, against whom the plagues were directed. Moving on, between the columns, into the Central Section, on the left is a figure of the baboon god Thoth, god of wisdom and writing; this is of the 18th Dynasty, about 1400 BC.

In the centre immediately behind the colossal head and arm is the red granite monument of Thutmose III (No EA 12). On the two sides are representations of the god Montu, with the king, headless, in between; on the two ends the goddess Hathor is represented. The king is identified in a cartouche on the belt and the others by columns of inscription above.

This brings to mind a saying of the late Rev L T Pearson, that the Bible says of the Children of Israel: "And I sent the hornet before you, which drave them out from before you, even the two kings of the Amorites; but not with thy sword, nor with thy bow" (Joshua 24 v 12). By the reign of Thutmose III, Egypt controlled an empire which encompassed Syria and Palestine in the north and Nubia in the south. "The sign of Thutmose was the hornet" (*The Bible Comes Alive*, Sir Charles Marston, Eyre & Spottiswoode).

18th DYNASTY FIGURES

Opposite on the right is a limestone figure of **Amenophis I** of the 18th Dynasty (EA 683).

Passing into the Central Section, to the left is a limestone bust of **Ahmes**, queen of Amenophis I, wearing the Hathor wig (EA 93).

Opposite and facing is a quartzite head of **Amenophis III** of the Amarna period, 18th Dynasty (EA 6).

Between the glass cases in front of us are three figures of the 18th Dynasty period.

Further on again to the left are two very fine figures of a man and wife of the 18th Dynasty period.

Opposite to these, on the right, may be seen a red granite head of **Amenophis III**, and a black granite head also of the 18th Dynasty (EA 119 and 526).

CENTRE CASES: JEWELS AND GODS

In these centre cases are many figures of the gods of Egypt and other items of interest. The gold and other jewellery in these remind us of the time when the Children of Israel left Egypt, for God had said, "And I will give this people favour in the sight of the Egyptians: and it shall come to pass, that when ye go, ye shall not go empty: but every woman shall borrow of her neighbour, and of her that sojourneth in her house, jewels of silver, and jewels of gold, and raiment: and ye shall put them upon your sons, and upon your daughters; and ye shall spoil the Egyptians" (or Egypt). The word translated "borrow" here means to ask, and evidently the Egyptians willingly gave jewellery and raiment to the Israelites. This gold, silver and cloth was later willingly offered for the construction of the Tabernacle in the Wilderness. The bronze mirrors of the women were used in the construction of the Laver, which itself speaks of the cleansing "with the washing of water by the word". In James 1 v 23 the word of God is likened to a mirror in which a man may see himself. Even these exquisite pieces of jewellery can turn our thoughts to God and to His word and purposes.

The gods of Egypt represented throughout these galleries were proved to be entirely powerless to avert the judgements of the God of Israel on the land and people which they were supposed to protect.

EA 64391 is a bronze cat sacred to the god Bastet; EA 6006 a gilded silver figure of Amen-Re; EA 1238 the head of a king of the 18th Dynasty (which may be Thutmose II); EA 65401 gold foil figure of god Ptah; EA 65329 gold pendant figure of god

Amun; also here gold pendant amulets with goddess Mut and god Thoth. EA 7853 is a pectoral with Anubis; EA 11054 a bronze of Osiris; EA 34954 a group of Isis and other deities; EA 60857 bronze head of goddess Isis; EA 11143 a bronze figure of the goddess Sothis, personification of the dog star, Sirius.

This gives us an illustration of the perversion of God's purposes by heathenism beginning with Nimrod, who built a tower whose top was "unto heaven", not to reach to heaven: this was the beginning of astrology which has such a vogue today.

Psalm 19 v 1 says, "The heavens declare the glory of God" and v 3, "There is no speech or language where their voice is not heard." In the stars, with their ancient Hebrew names, is written the story of the Redemption and Judgement: this has been perverted into heathen mythology.

The name of **Sirius** in Hebrew means "**The Prince**" (SR), as in Isaiah 9 v 6. Other stars in this constellation are called by names meaning "Who shall come", "The Prince or Chief of the Right Hand" and "The Mighty". Here there is no conflicting voice; no discord in the harmonious testimony to Him whose Name is called "Wonderful, Counsellor, the Mighty God, the Prince of Peace". Hence Sirius is, as we see it, the brightest star in the heavens. (See *The Witness of the Stars* by Dr E W Bullinger.)

To continue with the figures in the centre cases, EA 12587 is a bronze figure of the moon god I-Ah; EA 64532 a ram figure of god Khnum: EA 11498 a bronze hawk-headed deity; EA 25261 is a bronze figure of the god Ptah. Two more bronze figures represent the gods Khons Nefornotep and Nefertum, Nos EA 52945 and EA 64480 respectively. In the left hand case is a bronze kneeling figure of **Taharqua**, No EA 6395. (This is the Tirhakah of Isaiah 37 v 9.) Also in the left hand case is the bronze kneeling figure of an unnamed king offering before the sacred Aphis-bull, EA 22920.

Past the cases on the right is a head of **Amenophis III** of the Amarna period, EA 7.

Opposite, on the left, is a bust of the goddess Mut, EA 948, also of the period of the 18th Dynasty.

Between the columns at the entrance to the northern end of the gallery are, on the left, a limestone figure holding a shrine with representations of the gods Horus, Osiris and the goddess

Isis, EA 1377; this figure is of an overseer of the treasury of the 19th Dynasty, about 1250 BC, an ancient Chancellor of the Exchequer: in the centre is a black granite sacred boat decorated with representations of the goddess Hathor and with the seated statue of the mother of Amenophis III upon it. On the right is a wooden statue of **Rameses I** of the 19th Dynasty, about 1318 BC.

Entering the northern end of the Sculpture Gallery we see on the wall on the left the stela of Horemheb. The future king worships Re-Harakhty, Thoth and Maat, EA 551. Opposite on the right is the upper part of a red granite figure of **Rameses II** with the emblems of Osiris, the crook and flail, wig of curls and double crown, EA 67.

Moving on, we stand in front of the colossal head of **Rameses II**; this head weighing some 12 tons, is executed in two colour granite cleverly used to differentiate between the head and the body. During the Napoleonic expedition an attempt had been made to remove this head from Thebes, but it was not until 1816 that Belzoni succeeded in moving it and arranging for its transportation to London, where it was put on display in 1818. It has become widely accepted by Egyptologists and scholars that Rameses II was the Pharaoh of the oppression. This has also been widely accepted by the evangelical world despite its obvious opposition to the Bible record.

To the left of this colossal head are two red granite figures of Rameses II, and one of limestone. One, showing the king wearing the double crown of Upper and Lower Egypt and holding the crook and flail, signs of royal power, comes from the temple of the Nile Cataract deity, the ram-headed Khnum. The other came from the temple of the cat-goddess Bastet at Bubastis. By his side the king holds a staff which originally had a cult figure mounted upon it. The third figure of Rameses II is a limestone kneeling statue of the king holding a table of offerings. Next to this, a quartzite seated figure of king **Sethos II** holding on his knees a small shrine topped with a ram's head, the ram being one of the physical manifestations of Amun, the imperial god of Thebes.

Behind the head of Rameses II are five representations of the gods of Egypt: the Horus-falcon (EA 1420); the baboon-god Thoth (EA 1232–3); the god of wisdom and writing, also sacred to the moon deity Khons; the goddess Thoeris as a hippopotamus, patroness of women in childbirth (EA 1006); and a falcon inscribed to represent the solar-god Re-Harakhty.

Past the entrance to the side gallery and across the centre is the granite sphinx of **Taharqua** (Tirhakah), EA 1770, and the granite ram of Amun with the figure of Taharqua in protection between its paws. The worship of Amun was introduced into Ethiopia by the Egyptians and the ram became the most venerated object of the Kushite kings.

Opposite with back to the left-hand wall is a statue of the Nile god Hapi. This figure has the features of **Osorkon I** with, in relief, his son Sheshonq (Shishak) on the side.

Next to Hapi is another representation of Sakhmut, the leonine goddess of destruction; this is inscribed to Sheshonq. It is said that it was to this goddess that the people appealed for water when in the first of the plagues the waters were turned to blood, but as with the prophets of Baal on Mount Carmel beseeching "O Baal, hear us," there was no voice that answered.

Across the gallery on the opposite wall is the black basalt **Shabaka Stone**. It is thought that **Shabaka** is the **So** of the Bible. This stone has on it a text of the creation of the world (EA 498). This was ordered by So to preserve its contents for eternity; it was later used as a mill-stone.

Shishak was the one who, in the time of **King Rehoboam**, came against Jerusalem and took away the treasures of the house of the Lord. So was the king of Egypt with whom Hoshea, king of Israel, made a conspiracy against Shalmaneser of Assyria, which led to him being bound in prison by the king of Assyria and ultimately to the downfall of Samaria and the deportation of the ten tribes of the nothern kingdom of Israel.

Further on the right-hand wall is a statue of Isis and Osiris (EA 1162); this statue was dedicated by Shishak.

We now face two granite columns with palm leaf capitals. Both were initially inscribed in the reign of Rameses II, but later the name of Osorkon was added to the one on the left and that of Merneptah to the one on the right.

In the British Museum Guide C, p247, it says that on the monolith of Merneptah found by Petrie in 1896 is a mention of the Israelites. Although not the only translation, Dr Pinches in *The Old Testament in the Light of Historical Records* states that it has been translated to mean, "Jenoam has been brought to nought; Israel the horde, destroyed his crops."

Placed centrally between the granite columns and the two obelisks almost at the northern end of the gallery is the great granite scarab. The scarab-beetle was the creature associated with the god Khepri, the form of the sun-god Re at the time of his birth in the morning. It seems incredible that a beetle should represent such a luminary as the sun, but such is the depravity of the mind of man. The great scarab-beetle is EA 74 and is of the Ptolemaic period 200 BC.

On the wall on the right is a sandstone stela of Domitian, Roman emperor 81–96 AD (EA 709). The emperor, as Pharaoh, makes an offering to Buchis the bull. Domitian was an early persecutor of the Church and it was probably he who banished the apostle John to Patmos.

Below on the left is a sandstone stela of Tiberius Caesar. Here again the emperor, as Pharaoh, kneels before the goddess Mut and her son (EA 398). The text commemorates the making of the statue of Mut and the restoration of buildings connected with her sanctuary at Karnak. Tiberius was Caesar during our Lord's ministry.

On the right between the two granite columns and the great scarab is the northern entrance to the side gallery. Entering here and turning left, we see at the end a case with representations of the gods of Egypt. In the case to the right is a piece, EA 24429, dated in the 15th year of Shabaka (So of the Bible), 702 BC; this is the highest year recorded for So. EA 153 is a deified Thutmose III offering to the god Amun, his wife the goddess Mut and their son Khons, and to the goddess Hathor. Amenophis I is also represented here.

FIRST AND SECOND EGYPTIAN ROOMS

Leaving the gallery at the northern end, we mount the stairs into the Second Egyptian Room, turn left, and we are in the First Egyptian Room. These two rooms are given over to mummies, mummy cases, coffins and mummified remains of animals representative of various gods. On the left of the doorway of the First Egyptian Room are Wall Cases Nos 1, 2, 3 and 4 containing mummified bodies of animals, and mummy cases of wood and bronze mainly typical of various gods, such as cat, crocodile, jackal, falcon, etc.

Case 14 contains a papyrus document, No Pap 10561, written in Demotic script and dated the 12th July 157 BC. This is a document defining which persons should be employed in the various ceremonies of mummification. Evidently disputes over who does what are not new, for this document was the settlement of a demarkation dispute: is there anything "new under the sun"? (Ecclesiastes 1 v 9).

The main areas of these two rooms are filled with mummies, coffins and cases of men, women and children. One cannot help but wonder at the amazing workmanship and designs on these objects.

These have relevance to the Bible story, for in Genesis 49 we read that Jacob charged his sons saying, " . . . bury me with my fathers in the cave that is in the field of Ephron the Hittite, in the cave that is in the field of Machpelah in the land of Canaan, which Abraham bought . . . for a possession of a burying place." Then in chapter 50, verse 2, "And Joseph commanded his servants the physicians to embalm his father: and the physicians embalmed Israel."

Some hundreds of years later when the Children of Israel were delivered from bondage in Egypt, the remains of Joseph went with them. As Joseph was dying he "took the oath of the Children of Israel, saying, 'God will surely visit you, and he shall carry up my bones from hence.' So Joseph died, being an hundred and ten years old; and they embalmed him, and he was put in a coffin in Egypt" (Genesis 50 vv 25–26).

Exodus 13 v 19 says, "And Moses took the bones of Joseph with him . . ." Acts 7 vv 15–16 would seem to indicate that not only Jacob's and Joseph's remains were mummified and buried in the land of Israel, but also those of all the brethren, for it reads, "So Jacob went down into Egypt and died, he, and our fathers, and were carried over into Sychem, and laid in the sepulchre that Abraham bought for a sum of money of the sons of Emmor, the father of Sychem." All this is brought vividly to mind as we look at the mummies and coffins in these two rooms.

THIRD EGYPTIAN ROOM

The long wooden partition in the Third Egyptian Room has displayed upon it the Rhind Mathematical Papyrus. This is of the Hyksos period about 1575 BC; it is a copy of an even earlier document of 1850 BC. The papyrus begins with arithmetical problems mainly illustrating the multiplication and division of fractions, followed by methods of computing the volume and cubic contents of cylinders, measuring the area of a square, a circle, a triangle, and determining the slope of the sides of pyramids (No 10057).

Following on the central wooden partition is the London Medical Papyrus (No 10059). This contains spells and prescriptions for remedying burns and diseases affecting bones, eyes and female organs; it is of the 19th–20th Dynasty, about 1200 BC.

The diseases of Egypt have special mention in the Bible. It is said that Egyptian society was morally exceedingly corrupt, with all sorts of sexual excesses being practised.

In Deuteronomy, the Children of Israel are given a special promise and a solemn warning; the promise, if they follow the law of the Lord, and the warning if they depart from it. The promise is in Deuteronomy 7 v 15: "And the Lord will take away from thee all sicknesses, and will put none of the evil diseases of Egypt, which thou knowest, upon thee . . ." The warning is in Deuteronomy 28 v 60: "Moreover He will bring upon thee all the diseases of Egypt, which thou wast afraid of; and they shall cleave unto thee."

This would seem to have particular relevance in our day, for the truth of God does not change. Recently there has arisen this mysterious fatal disease, with no cure, which has its source in homosexuality but can be transmitted to others through blood transfusions: "for whatsoever a man soweth, that shall he also reap. He that soweth to the flesh . . . corruption; he that soweth to the Spirit . . . life everlasting" (Galatians 6 vv 7–8).

Following round to the left of the entrance into this room is Wall Case No 95. This contains figures representative of various gods, the ram, vulture, falcon, baboon, hippopotamus and tortoise.

In Case No 96 is a human-headed green jasper heart scarab in its original gold setting, inscribed for the Hyksos ruler Sobkemsaf, whose seated statue we saw in the lower gallery.

Cases Nos 98 and 99 contain various figures to accompany the dead.

Case No 111 has in it papyrus manuscripts. No 10685 is of particular interest, for it is a charm for dispelling a headache. The Egyptian term for headache is literally "half-head", translated in the Greek as Hemikranion; today we would say migraine or, significantly, a "splitting headache". As all will know, a headache is in the top of the skull or cranium. This

Bronze Mirror from Egypt: the Laver in the Tabernacle in the wilderness was made from the metal mirrors which the Israelite women brought from Egypt

Mass Production of Bread in Egypt

gives point to the meaning of the Greek word used in all the Gospels — Kranion, translated in Luke as Calvary and otherwise as Golgotha or "the place of a skull". As we may read in the section on General Gordon and the British Museum, the description has nothing to do with the seeming appearance of a skull face on the rock erroneously called "Gordon's Calvary", but means the top or head of the hill, which is Moriah. This place was designated as the place of the crucifixion by C R Conder some years before Gordon came to Palestine, and the tomb authenticating it was first discovered in 1867, some 16 years before Gordon's arrival. This only came to light on General Gordon setting enquiries going which resulted in the excavation of the tomb in 1891 by the German architect Conrad Schick.

The description of "Gordon's Calvary" is widely accepted today; so easily can a false tradition arise when the true facts are not known or perhaps passed over.

FOURTH EGYPTIAN ROOM

The Fourth Egyptian Room contains articles and scenes from everyday life in ancient Egypt. On entering the room, the wall cases on the left contain displays of basketry and rope, toilet articles, cosmetics, clothing and footwear in succession.

An article of interest amongst the toiletries is the bronze mirror with a wooden handle. It was from the bronze mirrors, which the Israelite women brought from Egypt, that the Laver in front of the Tabernacle in the Wilderness was made.

In the footwear section may be seen sandals with leather-thong fastenings. From the shape of the fastening came the Egyptian sign of life, and later one of the origins of the sign of the cross as a Christian symbol.

We are reminded here of the words of John the Baptist in reply to his questioners and regarding the Lord Jesus Christ, "He it is, who coming after me is preferred before me, the latchet of whose shoes I am not worthy to unloose." The word here translated "latchet" is the Greek word Himas, which means a thong or strap.

Continuing round the wall cases we come to spinning and weaving, magic in daily life, and in Case No 148 servants at work. Here a piece of interest is No 55730, bread making. A woman is grinding corn, a man kneading dough and another

Scribes recording the harvest in Egypt. (Gen. 41 vv 47–49) "And he gathered up all the food of the seven years, and laid up the food in the cities. And Joseph gathered corn as the sand of the sea, very much until he left numbering; for it was without number." (Gen. 41 vv 48–49)

Servant with basket of
bread and foodstuff on
her head (see page 95)

Photograph: BM

Brick with straw and Stamp of
Rameses II (see page 101)

Photograph: BM

94

woman baking, sitting in front of an oven and holding up a hand to shield her face from the heat.

Nos 45074–5 are figures with baskets of bread or fruit on their heads. Nos 30716 and 41673 are figures carrying baskets with bread and other foodstuffs on their heads.

In Genesis 40 vv 16–19 we read of the dream of Pharaoh's chief baker and Joseph's interpretation. The baker tells how in his dream he had on his head three baskets, and in the topmost one all manner of bakemeats for Pharaoh, and the birds did eat them out of the basket. Joseph predicts that within three days "Pharaoh shall lift up thy head from off thee." A Jewish friend tells me that the phrase "lift up" has the same derivation as the word used in the Gospel of John, where the Lord Jesus says, "I, if I be lifted up . . . will draw all unto me," signifying what death He should die.

Cases 150 and 151 have a representation of the mass production of bread, followed by navigation and in Cases 156–158 agriculture. No 50705 in this section is the Eastern one-handled plough. Luke 9 v 62: "And Jesus said unto him, No man, having put his hand to the plough, and looking back, is fit for the kingdom of God." Only one hand is mentioned, for as may be seen, the plough had only one handle; the other hand carried the long goad, mentioned to Saul on the Damascus road in Acts 9 v 5, ". . . it is hard for thee to kick against the pricks" (or goad). The goad was used to make a recalcitrant animal move in the right direction; even so had the Spirit of God been "pricking" Paul in his innermost spirit until finally he yielded in the words, "Lord, what wilt thou have me to do?"

In case 158 is a model of an Egyptian granary, which is a reminder of how Joseph caused the grain of the seven years of plenty to be stored against the lean years, which was ultimately to be the means of bringing the Children of Israel into Egypt.

Following round, other cases are devoted to weapons, houses and buildings, stone working and vessels, and scribes and artists. Items 178 and 179 have examples of scribes and materials. We see the ink horn, the pen case and brushes used in writing on papyrus.

Cases showing artists and craftsmen and furniture bring us to the door which was our starting point.

We now contemplate the displays in the centre cases.

Centre Case A, on the left, contains toilet objects. Pieces of interest are 30736, a bronze eye paint stick, and 63271, an alabaster kohl pot. It is recorded in 2 Kings 9 v 30 that Jezebel, the heathen wife of Ahab king of Israel, "painted her face and tired her head . . ." These articles are much before the time of Jezebel, so that the practice was nothing new in her day and still continues in ours. Also in this case are combs for "tiring" the hair.

There are several examples of razors here; they remind us that when Joseph was brought out of prison to interpret Pharaoh's dream, ". . . they brought him hastily out of the dungeon; and he shaved himself, and changed his raiment, and came in unto Pharaoh" (Genesis 41 v 14).

Here too are some fine examples of bronze mirrors, one of which No 22830, is highly polished. The size of these mirrors gives a better idea of the amount of metal given by the women for the making of the Laver which stood before the Tabernacle in the Wilderness.

Case B contains stringed instruments and music. No 20755 is a harp with the soundbox in the shape of a boat and No 6373 is a pair of bronze cymbals; also here are flutes and other items. Cymbals are mentioned sixteen times in the Old Testament in connection with praising the Lord.

Looking at these instruments brings vividly to mind the orchestra of king Nebuchadnezzar recorded in Daniel, "That at what time ye hear the sound of the cornet, flute, harp, sackbut, psaltery, dulcimer and all kinds of musick, ye fall down and worship the golden image that Nebuchadnezzar the king hath set up . . . " (Daniel 3 v 5).

Centre Case C contains toys and games. Children, it seems, have always played. The Lord Jesus used the illustration of children playing in the market place saying, "We have played at funerals and you have not lamented, we have piped and you would not dance." Zechariah 8 v 5 says, "And the streets of the city shall be full of boys and girls playing in the streets thereof." Children can still be seen darting in and out amongst the people thronging the streets of the Old City of Jerusalem.

Centre Case D deals with food and drink. No 45197 in this case is a further example of bread making and 36190 is a bowl of Egyptian wheat. We have previously seen a storehouse for wheat and here is an example of the grain itself. Nos 51091 and 22947 are representations of oxen ploughing with the one-handled plough, such as was seen in one of the wall cases. Deuteronomy 22 v 20 forbids ploughing with an ox and an ass together, and the New Testament warns Christians not to be unequally yoked together with unbelievers.

Case E is given over to navigation.

Case F displays weapons, one of which is an arrow with a reed shaft and a bronze head. There are many references to arrows in the Old Testament; we just mention one of them, Psalm 45 v 5, "Thine arrows are sharp in the heart of the king's enemies."

Case G contains foundation deposits, including an adze from the temple of Thutmose.

Case H has domestic equipment. In this case are a number of door keys. Keys are used figuratively in the New Testament, as in Revelation 1 v 18, "I am He that liveth, and was dead; and behold I am alive for evermore, Amen; and have the keys of hell and of death," and in Revelation 3 v 7, "These things saith He that is holy, He that is true, He that hath the key of David, He that openeth and no man shutteth; and shutteth and no man openeth." There are only two references to a key in the Old Testament, one in Judges and the other in Isaiah 22 v 22, to which the verse in Revelation is a direct reference, "And the key of the house of David will I lay upon His shoulder; so He shall open, and none shall shut; and He shall shut, and none shall open." Here again the key is being used prophetically and figuratively. A key as such is only mentioned once, and that is in Judges 3 v 25 where the servants of Eglon the king of Moab "took a key and opened the doors of the summer house," although verse 23 says that Ehud had locked the doors previously. We hardly imagine the ancients using keys such as we have, but before us is the evidence.

No 30874 is a pestle and mortar. Speaking of the manna in the wilderness, Numbers 11 v 8 says, "And the people went about and gathered it, and ground it in mills, or beat it in a mortar." Drinking vessels here may serve to remind us of Belshazzar's feast in Babylon, where the king made a great feast to a thousand of his lords, and drank wine before them. Belshazzar then commanded that the gold and silver vessels which Nebuchadnezzar, his father, had taken from the temple in Jerusalem might be brought in, that all might drink from them. Following this came the mysterious writing on the wall, which foretold the fate of the king, which Daniel interpreted (Daniel 5).

Lamps such as No 200785 were the "candle" of the Bible, and lampstands the "candlestick". Matthew 5 v 15: "Neither do men light a candle and put it under a bushel, but on a candlestick . . ."

Case I is labelled Mensuration (Measurement). In this case is a drawing of men going out with a measuring line. Zechariah 2 vv 1–2 reads: "I lifted up my eyes again and looked, and behold a man with a measuring line in his hand. Then said I, Whither goest thou? And he said unto me, To measure Jerusalem, and to see what is the breadth thereof, and what is the length thereof."

No. 6025 is a measuring rod or reed. Ezekiel 40 v 3: ". . . and behold, there was a man, whose appearance was like the appearance of brass, with a line of flax in his hand, and a measuring reed; and he stood in the gate." Here we have mentioned a measuring line and a reed or rod. The measuring reed mentioned here was probably about 10 feet in length, for verse 5 tells us that it was 6 cubits long by the cubit and a hand breadth. The mention of the "hand breadth" is of interest, as the "common cubit" was reckoned to be "six palms" in length. However, by the time of Ezekiel a second "long cubit" measuring seven palms was in use, which is calculated at just over 20 inches, so that the reed would have been 10 feet or so in length (*Pictorial Biblical Encyclopedia*). No 6025 therefore is of special interest as it is a cubit of seven palms with graduations.

No 37638 is a pottery plummet from a balance. Many scales in recent times had a metal pointer which when exactly corresponding to a mark on the scale showed that the balance was equal and the prescribed weight correct. The plummet, fixed on to a line, is still used in building, or even hanging paper, to show whether an exact vertical has been obtained. So in Isaiah 28 v 17 God says that He will test our righteousness by His plummet, and that will reveal that which is not true in His sight.

Case J is devoted to scribes and artists. Even fifty years ago Bible critics were raising the question, "Could Moses write?" The idea being to postulate a much later date for the Pentateuch; the suggestion was that writing was unknown in the time of Moses. Archaeology has long since shown the absurdity of such a notion.

In the case before us are examples of writing materials in use well before the time of Moses. No 12784 is a wooden palette with reed brushes and a stick for mixing ink; this is of the time of Amosis, the first king of the 18th Dynasty, 1570–1546 BC. Acts 7 v 22 tells us that ". . . Moses was learned in all the wisdom of the Egyptians." There can be no doubt at all that Moses could write. It is now recognised that Moses was copying from earlier written records in his accounts of the creation and events up to his own day.

Another interesting item is 5601, a wooden drawing board, and on it a figure of Thutmose III drawn in accord with canons of proportion: even graph paper is not new.

Nos 5512 and 36825 are paint boxes of 1450 BC. Nos 38145–6 are pointed reed pens; these are of the second century AD. It was not until Graeco-Roman times that pens were pointed; previously they were cut into a brush. This applied to the Hebrew scribes' pens also.

No. 43084 is a pen case with reed pens and an inkwell half full of black ink. The ink which the scribes used was not a thin liquid like modern ink but a viscid fluid made from oil, gum arabic and lamp black. The Hebrew scribes reputedly have secret formulae still used for writing the Scriptures.

Here also are Graeco-Roman wooden writing tablets with a wax covering. A pointed stylus was used for writing on these. These tablets were used for note taking and could be smoothed over and re-used. The tablets here are dated as 30 BC, so that such articles would have been commonly in use in Gospel times. A fine example of this is in Luke 1 v 63 where Zacharias, the father of John the Baptist, "asked for a writing table, and wrote, saying, His name is John."

Much older are the writing boards, such as No 5647, covered with gypsum plaster and dated 1450 BC. These were used like a slate for writing which could be rubbed off. Psalm 119 v 103 says, "How sweet are Thy words unto my taste. Yea, sweeter than honey to my mouth." This is a reflection of the practice of the rabbis to smear honey on the pupils' writing tablets which they could enjoy licking off.

Case K features script development. In this case are several letters in Coptic written by Egyptian Christians. Copt means Egyptian and the Egyptian Orthodox Church is called the Coptic Church; the ancient language of Egypt is preserved in the liturgy of the Coptic Church. No 32782 is a pastoral letter in Coptic from a bishop of the sixth century AD. Nos 21016,

Photograph: BM

Brick Making in Egypt (Exodus 5 vv 7 & 8)

21120 and 21201 are letters to an ecclesiastical superior asking for advice. No 14030 is a pottery fragment with the opening lines of psalms written upon it.

Case L contains tools. Examples of adze and axes may be seen in this case, also bronze bradawls and saws.

Speaking of graven images, the prophet Isaiah says, "The carpenter stretcheth out his rule; he marketh it out with a line; he fitteth it with planes, and he marketh it out with a compass, and maketh it after the figure of a man, according to the beauty of a man; that it may remain in the house. He heweth him down cedars . . ." (Isaiah 44 vv 13–17). Nos 6055 and 6044 are bronze bradawls. If a Hebrew bought a Hebrew slave he was to be given his liberty in the seventh year. If the man loved his master and did not want to leave, then his master was to bring him to the doorpost "and his master shall bore his ear through with an aul; and he shall serve him for ever." The bronze saws may remind us of Hebrews 11 v 37, "they were sawn asunder" and v 38, "of whom the world was not worthy." Tradition has it that Isaiah was thus executed.

At the other end of the room is the entrance to the Fifth Egyptian Room. Before entering we see in the wall cases to the right items of particular interest, showing the brick making process and examples of sun-dried bricks, some without and one with straw incorporated in the material.

The first case is the wooden model of brick makers at work. One man cuts Nile mud, another waits to take it to the brick makers, and a third is seen moulding the bricks in a rectangular wooden mould and placing them in lines to dry.

In the front of the case are examples of two bricks made without straw, Nos 13176 and 1752; these are of 1250 BC and 1000 BC.

No 6020 is a brick stamped with the name of Rameses II, c 1275 BC. This is much larger and the chopped-up straw can be clearly seen.

Up to recent times handmade bricks were produced in similar wooden moulds in this country, and certain types of specialist bricks are still so made. In many countries bricks continue to be made in this fashion. Only a few years ago, on a relief programme in southern Sudan, this method was used, and the bricks were air dried before firing in a huge clamp. These bricks were made from material from mud holes which must have been the same as the examples before us.

Bricks made thus are very prone to cracking and warping, and careful drying and turning is needed to avoid this. To overcome the problem, a non-plastic material such as straw, which does not shrink in the same way, is incorporated. This assists drying and also binds. As may be seen in the examples before us, the incorporation of straw allows much larger bricks to be produced, with the advantage of more rapid building and handling.

How vividly these bricks bring to our minds the picture of the Children of Israel in bondage in Egypt!

In Exodus 1 vv 13–14 we read, "And the Egyptians made the Children of Israel to serve with rigour: and they made their lives bitter with hard bondage, in mortar and in brick, and in all manner of service in the field: all their service wherein they made them serve was with rigour." And later in Exodus 5 vv 6–8, "And Pharaoh commanded the same day the taskmasters of the people, and their officers, saying, Ye shall no more give the people straw to make brick as heretofore: let them go and gather straw for themselves. And the tale of the bricks, which they did make heretofore, ye shall lay upon them; ye shall not diminish ought thereof: for they be idle; therefore they cry saying, Let us go and sacrifice to our God." And verse 10b and 11, "Thus saith Pharaoh, I will not give you straw. Go ye, get you straw where ye can find it: yet not ought of your work shall be diminished."

In the next case, No 166, are tools used in building. No 36881 is a builder's line, c 1300 BC, and 36754 a plumb bob, after 800 BC. Bricklayers still use the line and plumb bob when laying bricks. No 16036 is the bronze head of a hoe, probably for mixing mortar, also after 800 BC. Nowadays mortar is mixed in mechanical mixers, but not so long ago the brickies' labourer could be seen hurriedly mixing mortar with a shovel by hand and also carrying bricks and mortar to the layers in a hod. No 41195 in this case is a leather bag which was probably a mortar hod.

No 5409 is a trowel, c 1300 BC, and No 41187 a mason's mallet made of a dense heavy wood not yet identified, c 1300 BC.

FIFTH EGYPTIAN ROOM

We now enter the Fifth Egyptian Room. The cases here contain statuettes, heads and figures of kings, officials, people and deities of various areas and dynasties. Case No 209 has a representation of the crocodile god Sihek, No 37450. When Pharaoh ordered that all male babies born to the Israelites should be thrown into the Nile, they were in effect an offering to the gods. This makes all the more significant the fact that Moses, the one who later was to bring about the defeat of Pharaoh in the matter of the Hebrew slaves, should himself have been rescued from the river. Also in this case is the scorpion goddess Isis-Selik, No 11629, and two representations of Apis the bull.

Case No 216 has a figure of the god Bes or Baal; this figure is after 30 BC in the Roman period. Going back to case 213, we see the head of a cow sacred to the god Hathor, No 42179, reminding us again of the plague which fell on the Egyptian cattle. Cases 218–220 contain universal deities.

The centre cases here contain the same type of display as the wall cases.

SIXTH EGYPTIAN ROOM

Retracing our steps, we enter the Sixth Egyptian Room by a doorway on the south side of the Fourth Egyptian Room.

Turning left, in Wall Case No 23 are seals and scarab types. Seal No 37763 is of Amenophis I and Thutmose III. Nos 30772 and 15700 are of the Hyksos period.

In Case No 25 are royal scarabs: No 30500 is of the Hyksos king Khyan; there is also one of Hatshepsut, the co-regent with Thutmose III, another of Thutmose III, 1504–1450 BC, and one of Rameses II, 1304–1237 BC. Scarabs of the 21st–24th Dynasties include ones of Sheshonq (Shishak), Shabaka (So), Taharqua (Tirhakah) and Necho or No.

The remaining cases in this room are given up to small pottery of various periods, jewellery and bronze objects.

COPTIC CORRIDOR

Leaving the Sixth Egyptian Room by the doorway by which we entered and going across the Fourth Room, we enter the Coptic Corridor. The British Museum Guide of 1976 has this to say about the Copts: "The word 'Copt' was originally a designation for the indigenous population of Egypt, as distinct from foreign settlers, but it gradually came to be applied specifically to the Christian part of the population."

The teachings of Christianity were written in a new form of script called Coptic, which is really the ancient Egyptian language written in Greek letters, with the addition of a few signs from Demotic.

The purpose of the emphasis on the representation of the gods and goddesses of ancient Egypt has been to show how completely evil had subverted the mind of man. The primeval monotheism had long given way to polytheism with its multitude of gods. Heathenism held sway, not only in Egypt, but universally. Its degrading effect can be seen in the things at which we have been looking, probably as much as anything in the representation of the king worshipping the Aphis-bull — the highest rank of human achievement falling down and worshipping an animal. As the Bible says of men, ". . . Who changed the truth of God into a lie, and worshipped and served the creature more than the Creator, who is blessed for ever. Amen" (Romans 1 v 25).

The question may well be asked, "What was it that banished from the earth these ancient gods, whether of Egypt, Rome or Assyria?" The answer is the gospel; when Christ died, rose and ascended, Satan's kingdom fell. The gospel day has lasted for some two thousand years, but would seem to be rapidly drawing to a close as Satan makes his last desperate bid for the soul of man. The fruit of atheistic materialism and "science, falsely so called" may be seen throughout the earth in lawlessness, violence and superstition.

The prophecy of Jeremiah was fulfilled in the overthrow of heathenism. "Thus shall ye say unto them, The gods that have not made the heavens and the earth, even they shall perish from the earth, and from under these heavens" (Jeremiah 10 v11). The triumph of Calvary is plainly stated in Colossians 2 v 15,"Having spoiled principalities and powers, He made a shew of them openly, triumphing over them in it" (the Cross).

The universal resurgence of evil is forecast in 2 Timothy 3 vv 1–5: "This know also, that in the last days perilous times shall come, for men shall be lovers of their own selves, covetous, boasters, proud, blasphemers, disobedient to parents, unthankful, unholy, without natural affection, truce-breakers, false accusers, incontinent, fierce, despisers of those that are good, traitors, heady, high minded, lovers of pleasure more than lovers of God, having a form (or outward semblance) of godliness, but denying the power thereof (ie having an outward facade of religion, but without the inner transforming power of God): from such turn away."

104

Pharaoh pursuing the enemy in his chariot

Note

* It is now thought that the Hyksos rulers of Egypt were perhaps not in control of the country when Joseph came. This may be so but would not alter the fact that in later years the Semitic Hyksos rulers would have been sympathetic to the Children of Israel.

Also that the first king of the 18th Dynasty, who began to drive out the Hyksos, would have been the king who knew not Joseph.

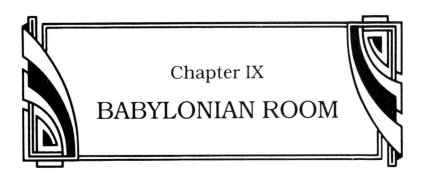

Chapter IX

BABYLONIAN ROOM

From the Fifth Egyptian Room, the Babylonian Room is entered. The displays in this room are of particular interest to us, as here may be seen artefacts found by Sir Leonard Woolley and others, from Ur of the Chaldees and places nearby. Abraham came from Ur of the Chaldees. Sir Leonard Woolley excavated for 12 years at Ur, 1922-1934.

"And Terah took Abram (Abraham) his son, and Lot the son of Haran his son's son, and Sarai (Sarah) his daughter-in-law, his son Abram's wife; and they went forth with them from **Ur of the Chaldees**, to go into the land of Canaan; and they came to Haran and dwelt there" (Genesis 11 v 31).

"Now the Lord had said unto Abram, Get thee out of thy country and from thy kindred, and from thy father's house, unto a land that I will shew thee" (Genesis 12 v 1).

The Sumerian name of Ur was Urim. Urim means "lights", so Ur means "light". In Exodus 28 v 30 we read of the Urim and Thummim which were to be put in the High Priest's breastplate, meaning lights and perfection. Just what these articles were is not known, but it was by means of these that God answered the High Priest.

"And God said, Let there be light, and there was light." Here God was using the same word for light in conjunction with the first syllable of His name Jehovah, "Yahi Or", "Let there be light" (or, There will be light); then follows the sublimest understatement of all time, "And there was light." (*The Wonders of the Hebrew Alphabet*, W E Steele-Smith.)

The first syllable of Jehovah is in the future tense. Naturally we speak of past, present and future, but God has no beginning or end, so that His name is future, present and past, a complete merging without beginning or end. How very sad it is to see that critical scholars have robbed God of His wonderful Name and substituted a meaningless "Yahweh" for the meaningful "Jehovah". This is a crime of the first magnitude: "Who steals my purse steals trash, but who steals my good name steals my most precious treasure." Let us not be guilty of this.

On entering the Babylonian Room, in the first wall case on the left, No 1, is the restored queen's harp and lyre, discovered by Woolley at Ur in 1927.

As we go round this room we may well wonder at the amazing skill of the craftsmen and the beauty of the objects which they produced. Such finds as these shatter for ever the notion that man has evolved to his present state of intelligence and that the more ancient the people, the less developed they were. The truth is that they did things which cannot be emulated today. They hardened copper to be as hard as steel, with a formula which scientists in our day have said is impossible. It has been said that craftsmen today cannot produce some of their fine workmanship and that we cannot, or find it difficult to, emulate some of their works based on mathematical calculations. The Babylonians had the Pythagorean numbers before 2000 BC. The evolution of man has not been up from darkness to light, but rather down from light to darkness.

In 2 Corinthians 4 v 4 the apostle says, "In whom the God of this world hath blinded the minds of them which believe not, lest the light of the glorious gospel of Christ, who is the image of God, should shine unto them," and v 6, "For God, who commanded the light to shine out of darkness, hath shined in our hearts, to give the light of the knowledge of the glory of God in the face of Jesus Christ."

Ephesians 6 v 12 tells us that "we wrestle not against flesh and blood, but . . . against the rulers of the darkness of this world . . ." The Lord Jesus said, "I am the light of the world: he that followeth me shall not walk in darkness, but shall have the light of life" (John 8 v 12).

In Wall Case No 2 are examples of glassware and glazed ware from Mesopotamia, from the late 16th and early 15th centuries BC. Of particular interest is item No 27, a tablet giving recipes for the manufacturing of various types of glass. Next to this are some samples of glass made from the recipes given on the tablet, some 3,500 years after they were written.

Wall Case No 3 contains dress and adornment. On the right in this case is a display of women's fashions 2000 BC–1500 BC, so that we are looking at dress in the time of Abraham.

In between Wall Cases 3–5 and Cases 5–7 are examples of inscribed Babylonian boundary stones. Deuteronomy 27 v 17 says, "Cursed be he that removeth his neighbour's landmark. And all the people shall say, Amen." These Babylonian landmarks also have inscribed upon them curses on anyone who moves them. In Palestine the stones marking out the Arab plots of land, seen in recent years, are not so heavy as these examples and so would be much more easily moved.

Wall Case No 5 contains Sumerian art from 3000 BC.

Wall Case No 7 has details of the excavations at Ur. Here are maps and illustrations of the various digs undertaken at the site of Ur. Prior to 1922 there had been limited excavations, but then Mr C L (afterwards Sir Leonard) Woolley led a large expedition for twelve seasons until 1934.

Here let us quote from the late Rev L T Pearson's book, *Through the Land of Babylonia.* "Kish. After a night's rest in the rail coach we set off next morning by cars a distance of fourteen miles, this time to visit Kish. This is the first city whose name appears in Sumerian inscriptions, and judging by archaeological discoveries, the date of its foundation appears to be 3100 BC. Here amidst remains of Nebuchadnezzar's time rises a well-preserved ziggurat."

The name implies "between earth and heaven". People lived below it, and on the summit had their temple shrine. It is solid and built of kilned bricks. Other ruins are immense and yet are but the lower storeys of the buildings. During excavations and amongst deeply interesting "finds" were discovered two chariot wheels of a very early period — in fact, the earliest wheels found in Iraq.

The lowest brickwork of the earliest date is the "plano-convex", and the date period of these bricks is 3100 BC. Kish was built 100 years after the Flood, so history tells us, and below this stratum of plano-convex bricks was found the silt bed of the Great Flood. (As may be expected, modern scholars dispute this.)

These plano-convex bricks were made from the flood silt and so were the first bricks after the Flood. This silt is an eight feet deep layer of pure water laid silt with no bones, pots or artefacts of any sort in it. Immediately underneath it could be found bones of men drowned in the Flood.

The tower mentioned in Genesis 11 vv 2–4 was built of such bricks made from the flood silt. It is generally assumed that these people were so ignorant that they thought that they could build a tower which would reach to heaven, but a careful look at the words in the AV Bible will show that the words "may reach" are in italics and therefore not in the original, so that the phrase reads, "whose top unto heaven". Its purpose was astrological, for with Nimrod and the Tower of Babel began astrology and the root of idolatry.

At Birs Nimrud are the remains of this tower composed of intensely hard vitrified brick, so hard and dense that it cannot be broken. Attempts were made by soldiers to break off pieces from the mass with sledgehammer and chisel, but without success.

As we know, Nebuchadnezzar was a great builder in brick. He appears to have done his utmost to level any city built before his time and to rebuild on the same site; but when it came to this tower, it could not be moved. He therefore covered up the old tower by building all round it and erecting his own tower on the top.

Again Leonard Pearson is quoted: "Near the summit of the mound, upon which he built his tower, one finds a curious rock-like substance, the original tower. Strike it with a tool and it rings like metal. Examine it and a brick-like substance may be seen, but each brick is solidly welded into its mate, and all is so hard as to defeat any power less than dynamite to break it up."

In connection with this, Leonard Pearson had an interesting story to tell of one whom he describes as the greatest brick expert in the world, and a convinced atheist. This man called on Leonard on a matter of business, and when finished he asked Leonard what his chief interest was. Leonard replied, the Bible. This brought forth a most scornful reply. Leonard then asked his visitor what his interest was. He said that he travelled the world selecting clays for industrial purposes. He was then shown a piece of the Birs Nimrud tower and asked if he would ever believe that it had been a brick. (In these pieces can be seen the join of what had once been two bricks, but the bricks have now shrunk to one half-inch or less.) The clay expert's answer was to the effect that this had never been a brick. Leonard then said that he supposed the expert knew that such bricks were set to dry on palm leaves. The man became impatient: "Of course I do." Turning the piece over, Leonard showed him the unmistakable pattern of the palm leaf made when the brick was still plastic. On being asked for his reaction the expert said, "When we scientists cannot explain anything we say it was an act of God." "But," said Leonard, "you have been denying the existence of God."

This, of course, is exactly what it was, for in Genesis the story continues, "And the Lord said, Behold the people is one, and they have all one language; and this they begin to do: and now nothing will be restrained from them, which they have imagined to do. Go to, let us go down, and there confound their language that they may not understand one another's speech. So the Lord scattered them abroad from thence upon the face of all the earth, and they left off to build the city. Therefore is the name of it called Babel . . ."

The confusion of the language is in the Bible story, but what about the vitrification of the mound? The only explanation which can be given is that the Lord so dealt with this mass in the fire of judgement as to make it immovable and a picture for all time of his displeasure — an act of God.

When Sir Henry Rawlinson excavated at Birs Nimrud, he found inscriptions left by Nebuchadnezzar, which are indeed helpful and explanatory: "The house of the earth's base, the most ancient monument of Babylon I built and finished. I exalted its head with bricks covered with copper, the house of the Seven Lights (the seven planets); a former king forty-two ages ago built, but did not complete its head. Since a remote time people had abandoned it, without orders expressing the words, the earthquake and the thunder had split and dispersed its sun-dried clay."

The Rev Pearson also used to quote a tablet of Nebuchadnezzar as saying, "In ancient times the gods came down and destroyed the tower. I restored it to its original purpose (astrological)."

"How can this mass of vitrified brick of the original tower be accounted for? Under intense heat the bricks were literally fused and then cooled into this rock-like slag. Was this achieved by the original builders who said, 'Go to, let us make brick and burn them thoroughly'? The answer is no, for there is no heat on earth that can be generated which could do it today (c1939). Could lightning have done it (the suggestion of modern archaeologists)? Again the answer is no. The whole of this mass rises about 200 feet above the plain and covers some 10 acres, the inner core solid through from top to bottom and the whole mass vitrified."

Again from Leonard Pearson: "Birs Nimrud by tradition has been associated with Nimrod the hunter and in Genesis 10 vv 8–10 we read, 'And Cush begat Nimrod: he began to be a mighty one in the earth. He was a mighty hunter before the Lord. And the beginning of his kingdom was Babel . . . in the land of Shinar' (Babylonia). Here is Nimrod linked with Babel, so the question is, 'Could this be the Tower of Babel?'"

Once more to Leonard Pearson: "Fools step in where angels fear to tread, and the writer does not mind being a fool in this respect, especially as archaeologists are less than angels, great men though they be. The archaeologist is a scientist and reserves his opinion until he has full evidence for any statement he makes (sic. Ed.). Whereas the scientist says, 'May be,' perhaps the mere student of the Bible may assert his convictions (ie that this is indeed the site of the Tower of Babel). It is so easy to say that the Tower of Babel lay within Babylon, seeing that the ziggurat of Babylon has altogether passed away (having been destroyed by Alexander the Great) and cannot be studied on the spot."

Reading on into the Rev L T Pearson's book *Through the Land of Babylonia*, we reach chapter four — "Ur of the Chaldees". "However interesting we have found Birs Numrud, Babylon and Kish, they have but whetted the appetite for our next thrill — Ur, the birthplace of Abraham.

"After a night's stop in the train, we find ourselves halted amongst a few buildings and on a board we read, 'Ur Junction'. After breakfast we set out and a twenty minute walk brings us into the ruins of this once famous city, and rising above the brick remains stands the immense ziggurat, the most perfect in Mesopotamia.

"Five thousand tons of debris were piled up against the ziggurat alone; this accumulation had all to be sifted, otherwise valuable relics would have been lost. The original temple on the top was dedicated to the Moon-god.

"The first to investigate Ur was Mr J E Taylor in 1854 when he was vice-consul at Basra, and until then no one dreamed that this brick heap, named by the Arabs Mugayyar, was the birthplace of Abraham."

Taylor dug at the four corners of the ziggurat and found inscribed cylinders. Just before this, the key to the cuneiform writing had been discovered and so the writing on the cylinders was deciphered. These four cylinders of Nabonidus, king of Babylonia, each contain the same text, and in the second column make mention of Belshazzar his eldest son and co-regent.

This part of the text reads: "As for me, Nabonidus, the king of Babylon, preserve me from sinning against thy great divinity, and grant me the gift of a life of long days; and plant in the heart of Bilu-Sarra-Utsur (Belshazzar), the eldest son, the offspring of my heart, reverence for thy great divinity, and never may he incline to sin; with fulness of life may he be satisfied" (*Fresh Light from the Ancient Monuments*, Professor A H Sayce, RTS 1892).

Thus again is the Bible record vindicated, and most interestingly so, in Daniel 5 v 7, where Belshazzar promises that whoever can read the writing on the wall and show the interpretation of it shall be made the "third ruler in the kingdom". Why not the second ruler? (Joseph was made second after Pharaoh.) The reason was that Belshazzar himself was the second, being co-regent with his father Nabonidus. More of this when we come to the Babylonian weights.

To return to Ur, Sir Leonard Woolley and the Flood. The Sumerian scribes had a king list which gives the names of kings who reigned "before the Flood". "And then the Flood came. After the Flood kingship was sent down from on high."

Whilst Sir Leonard was convinced by the evidence of a flood "unparalleled in any later period of Mesopotamian history," he did not accept the Genesis account of a universal inundation.

As at Kish, the silt of the Flood was also found at Ur up to 11 feet in depth. Sir Leonard tells us how, in 1929, a shaft was being sunk in the royal cemetery of Ur, when the Arab workman at the bottom announced that he had reached virgin soil and that there was nothing more to be found. Woolley was not satisfied and told the man to go on digging, which he did with great reluctance. After 8 feet of this pure water laid silt there appeared implements and fragments of pottery. He says that he was quite convinced of what it all meant but wanted to hear what the others thought. Two members of the staff had no idea what to say, but when his wife came along and was asked what she thought about it, "she turned away remarking casually, 'Well, of course, it's the Flood.'" (Sir Leonard Woolley, *Excavations at Ur*. Ernest Benn Limited. London, 1963.)

However, Sir Leonard maintains only a local flood of great extent, but he does say, on page 34 of his book, "The Flood was for the Sumerian reader the only flood that really mattered — what we call Noah's Flood." He quotes the Bible as saying in Genesis that the waters rose to a height of 26 feet (page 36). But does Genesis 7 vv 19–20 say that? Most assuredly not. It states very definitely, "And the waters prevailed exceedingly upon the earth; and all the high hills, that were under the whole heaven, were covered." That does not sound very local. It goes on, "Fifteen cubits upward did the waters prevail, and the mountains were covered." It does not say that the waters were 26 feet deep but 26 feet over the top of everything in the world.

Of course, one might stagger at this and say, "What, 26 feet over the top of Mount Everest!" The answer is simple enough: Everest and such like were not there, because the world after the Flood was very different from the world before that event.

Evolutionary scientists base their theories on the false premise so clearly foretold in 2 Peter 3 vv 3–7. "Knowing this first, that there shall come in the last days scoffers . . . saying, Where is the promise of His coming? for since the fathers fell asleep, all things continue as they were from the beginning of the creation. For this they willingly are ignorant of, that by the word of God the heavens were of old, and the earth standing out of the water and in the water: whereby the world that then was, being overflowed with water, perished. But the heavens and the earth which are now, by the same word are kept in store, reserved unto fire against the day of judgment and perdition of ungodly men."

The significant words here are "all things continue as they were from the beginning of the creation." Evolutionary science is based on this assumption; carbon dating, for instance, is based on a constant emission of carbon particles for the ages of time. Also the words "the world that then was" and "the heavens and the earth which are now" show a clear distinction between the pre and post Flood world.

In case it is thought that these are the ravings of a religious enthusiast, please read *The Genesis Flood* by Whitcombe and Morris and *Bone of Contention* by Sylvia White MSc.

Continuing with Wall Case No 8. Here are also electrotypes of gold objects from the royal graves at Ur; the originals found by Sir Leonard Woolley are now in the Iraq Museum, Baghdad (c2600 BC).

In the centre is a representation of a Sumerian shrine. On the first upright is a tablet with a hymn in cuneiform (No 96739). This hymn is to the Sumerian goddess Inanna (Ishtar to the Babylonians), the goddess of love and war, to be sung to the accompaniment of kettle drums.

Wall Case No 10 has the first objects from the temple of the goddess Nin-Hursasc, from Al 'Ubaid near Ur (c2600 BC).

Wall Case No 11, "Government", contains various articles, tools, arrow heads, spear heads, daggers and spears.

Wall Case No 12, "Trade and Transport". Much trade and transport was conducted by water on the rivers Tigris and Euphrates. Here are models of boats, a chariot drawn by onagers, which has solid wheels, and an ox-sledge. The sledge was used for transport over the desert or loose dirt roads.

Of particular interest are the weights in this case, the mina (No 116) divided into 60 shekels. We immediately think of the writing on the wall at the feast of Belshazzar and Daniel's interpretation thereof.

Daniel's interpretation showed that the solemn message had to do with weighing and measuring. "And this is the writing that was written, MENE, MENE, TEKEL, UPHARSIN. This is the interpretation of the thing: MENE; God hath numbered thy kingdom and finished it. TEKEL: Thou art weighed in the balances and art found wanting. PERES: Thy kingdom is divided and given to the Medes and Persians" (Daniel 5 vv 25–28). "In that night was Belshazzar the king of the Chaldeans slain. And Darius the Median took the kingdom, being about three-score and two years old" (vv 30–31).

Whilst the king was feasting, the enemy, having successfully diverted the water of the river, entered the city by the undefended Water Gate, without opposition.

The writing itself was a play on words: "Parsu or Barsu in Assyrian means a part of a shekel. Mane is the equivalent alike of the weight and the verb 'manu' to reckon. Peres or Parsu, a part of a shekel, comes from the root which signifies to divide, whilst the name of Persia is written in precisely the same manner in Babylonian and in Arabic."

Unbelieving criticism has dismissed the Book of Daniel as

quite unhistorical and Belshazzar as a figment of the imagination. Sir Charles Marston in his book *The Bible Comes Alive* (Eyre and Spottiswoode, 1938, p127) has this to say: "Without taking account of their limited knowledge of the period, and relying on classical history, some critics and commentators used to deny that Belshazzar ever existed. The classics told them that Nabonidus was the last king of Babylon. Hundreds and even thousands of cuneiform tablets of the period have now been found in Babylonia. Their evidence established the fact that Belshazzar was made a co-regent with Nabonidus, his father, in the third year of the latter's reign; they further suggest that Belshazzar's mother was probably the daughter of Nebuchadnezzar (which explains verse 2 of Daniel 5). And lastly they demonstrate that this chapter of Daniel excels all classical and other historical accounts in its knowledge of the period."

Wall Case No 13 has terracotta plaques showing gods and goddesses of 2000 to 1500 BC, Abraham's period. The Sumerians worshipped a great number of gods and goddesses, and passed on many to the Babylonian Semites who succeeded them. Reference is made to this in Joshua 24 v 14, "Now therefore fear the Lord, and serve Him in sincerity and in truth: and put away the gods which your fathers served on the other side of the flood, and in Egypt; and serve the Lord." Here "the other side of the flood" means the river, before Abraham crossed over to enter Canaan.

As has already been noted, Sumerian priests offering sacrifices in earlier times usually did so naked. Amongst the various plaques, models and figurines in this case is a representation of one so doing.

This is in direct contrast to the instructions given to Moses in Exodus 28 v 42 concerning Aaron and those who should "minister unto me in the priest's office". God says, "And thou shalt make them linen breeches to cover their nakedness; from the loins even unto the thighs they shall reach: and they shall be upon Aaron and upon his sons, when they come into the tabernacle of the congregation, or when they come near unto the altar to minister in the holy place."

From what we have seen in our tour of the Museum, it is obvious that heathenism is completely sexually immoral, pornographic and debased. 2 Timothy 1 v 10 says, ". . . our Saviour Jesus Christ, who hath abolished death, and hath brought life and immortality to light through the gospel." The word here translated "immortality" does not mean "deathlessness" but "incorruption". Despite the wonder of the law it could never banish heathenism, for the Children of Israel deserted the holy law and sank back into worshipping idols repeatedly until they were banished from the land. The law can only show what is sin, but has no power to abolish sin. The apostle says in Romans 7: "Wherefore the law is holy, and the commandment holy, and just and good." He says that he "had not known sin, but by the law: for I had not known lust except the law had said, Thou shalt not covet."

In Romans 8 he goes on to say, "For what the law could not do in that it was weak through the flesh, God sending His own Son in the likeness of sinful flesh, and for sin, condemned sin in the flesh; that the righteousness of the law might be fulfilled in us who walk not after the flesh, but after the Spirit." Martin Luther called the Epistle to the Romans, "The purest Gospel", and this is indeed the Good News of the Gospel.

The promise of God had been there all the time, long before it was made a reality in the coming, death and resurrection of the Son of God, for in Jeremiah 31 v 33 we read, "But this shall be the covenant that I will make with the house of Israel: After those days, saith the Lord, I will put my law in their inward parts, and write it in their hearts; and will be their God, and they shall be my people."

Wall Case No 14, "Daily Life". Here are toys, terracotta plaques and inscriptions. Three of the plaques show the very ancient motif of "Mother and Child". These are of the period 2000–1500 BC.

Wall Case No 15 contains bricks and stela.

Wall Case No 16, "Architecture and Furniture". In this case are to be seen inscribed clay "nails" or "cones". These were embedded in the masonry of buildings and were inscribed with details of the builder or restorer and the occasion. Here also are models, tablets and figurines. No 91071 is a clay cone of Hammurabi (Amraphel) recording the rebuilding of Sippar, about 1760 BC.

Wall Case No 17 contains statuettes and terracotta plaques of animals, wild and domesticated, dog, ox, goat and pig. The pig was domesticated in early times.

Here also is a saddle quern and a rolling stone pin (Nos 12728 and 127833) used in milling grain before the

The Standard of Ur

117

introduction of the rotary mill. Other examples were seen in the Egyptian Galleries.

Item No 14627 is a Sumerian tablet of about 2100 BC recording the issue of mill-stones from the storehouse to the mill and kitchen. We should call the storehouse a warehouse, which makes it all seem so up to date.

Wall Case No 18 contains a silver lyre found in 1927 by Sir Leonard Woolley at Ur. On a decorated box in one of the centre cases called the Standard of Ur, is an illustration of a musician playing a similar lyre.

Leaving the wall cases and turning to the right, we come to a centre case with articles illustrating the superb art of the Sumerians in gold and silver of around 2600 BC. No 122200, listed as a he-goat, used to be described as "a ram caught in a thicket", bringing to mind the incident of Abraham's sacrifice in Genesis 22 v 13.

Here also are daggers, gold cups and bowls, a strainer, a copper and gold axe, a spear head and strangest of all, gold chisels. The question might be asked, "Is it possible today to so harden gold that it can be used to make chisels?"

The next centre case has a build-up of the queen's sledge of about 2600 BC, made to slide on sand or loose soil trails.

In the middle centre case is the box already mentioned, known as the Standard of Ur, of about 2500 BC. The purpose of this hollow box is not certain, but it may have been a sound-box for a musical instrument.

The decoration on it shows a successful campaign by a king of Ur. The two ends have figures of animals and other scenes. In the right-hand top register is a musician accompanying a singer on a lyre similar to the one in Wall Case No 18.

Round to the left of this case is a terracotta relief of a female goddess with the feet of a hind, probably Lilith. No 120000 next to this is a drinking trough with sculpture in low relief, possibly a model. The sculpture illustrates a reed hut, such as may still be seen in the marshes of South Iraq, with symbols of the goddess Inanna (Ishtar) on the pole heads. Lambs run to meet the returning herds.

In the last centre case before the door is early Sumerian jewellery of gold and silver work and semi-precious stones. No 122294, in a small case at the back, is a crushed skull of one of the women attendants with the original jewellery, the skull crushed by the weight of earth upon it.

118

Chapter X
THE ROOM OF WRITING

Returning to the Sixth Egyptian Room, we enter the Room of Writing. Facing us as we enter is the India House Inscription, so called as originally it was displayed in India House, London. This is an inscription of Nebuchadrezzar, king of Babylon (Nebuchadnezzar), describing the building of temples and his own royal palace in Babylon. Whilst we may not be able to read it, the consideration of the technical excellence of this beautiful piece of craftsmanship is worthwhile.

Displayed on the wall to the left of the doorway are a number of ancient bricks with the royal stamps upon them.

No 14 is a brick of Hammurabi (Amraphel), 1792–1750 BC. No 1100: Tiglath-Pileser, 1115–1077 BC. Nos 25 and 58 bear the stamp of Ashurnasirpal, 884–859 BC. Nos 24, 34 and 54: Shalmaneser III, 859–824 BC. Bricks Nos 29, 38 and 55: Sargon II, 722–705 BC. Nos 30, 56 and 57 are from the reign of Sennacherib, 705–681 BC. No 40 is of Esarhaddon, 681–669 BC, the successor of Sennacherib. This brick also bears the name of Ashurbanipal, 669–627 BC, the successor of Esarhaddon. Nos 36 and 41 have stamps of two more kings who reigned before the fall of Nineveh in 612 BC.

Brick No 58 is of Merodach-Baladan, 721–710 BC. This was the king of Isaiah 39 vv 1–2, who "sent letters and a present to Hezekiah (king of Judah): for he had heard that he had been sick, and was recovered. And Hezekiah was glad of them and showed them . . . all that was found in his treasures: there was nothing in his house, nor in all his dominion, that Hezekiah shewed them not." As a result of that Isaiah said to Hezekiah, "Hear the word of the Lord of hosts: Behold, the days come, that all that is in thine house, and that which thy fathers have laid up in store until this day, shall be carried to Babylon:

119

Babylonian Cuneiform Tablet — mathematical problems and water clocks formulae (see page 135)

Brick inscribed with the name and titles of Nebuchadnezzar II. King of Babylon (c.605–562 B.C.)

nothing shall be left, saith the Lord." All this was not to happen in the lifetime of Hezekiah; it was in the ninth year of Zedekiah that Nebuchadrezzar (Nebuchadnezzar) came and destroyed Jerusalem and Solomon's temple and carried the treasures away to Babylon, with the people. The temple treasures do not reappear until we read of them being brought out at the feast of Belshazzar in the time of Daniel.

Bricks No 26, 37 and 53 are of the reign of Nebuchadrezzar, 605–562 BC. Nos 28 and 29 are bricks of Nabonidus, king of Babylon, 556–539 BC, the father of Belshazzar.

Following on in the wall cases are seals of Western Asia from 3500 BC. Notice the almost incredible work seen on these cylinder seals and on the impressions made by them.

Next in the case are stamp seals from before 3000 BC. These seals were used as marks of ownership and signatures on documents, contracts and deeds.

A small wall case has descriptions of the texts of the seals of Western Asia.

On the walls following are a number of inscriptions of very great interest; they are mostly casts, the originals being in other museums. Cast No 491 is of an inscription from the tomb of Hezir in the Kidron Valley, Jerusalem, wrongly called the Tomb of St James. Hezir was a priestly family of the first century AD.

In another tomb was found one of the few evidences known of crucifixion. This was an iron spike driven through a heel bone. Experts at the Hebrew University spent some two years examining these bones to try to find out the manner in which people were crucified.

It may come as a shock to know that there is no word such as "cross" in the Greek of the New Testament. The word translated "cross" is always the Greek word "staurus", meaning a "stake" or "upright pale". The cross was not originally a Christian symbol; it is derived from Egypt and Constantine. The arms of the victim were not extended, neither were the legs straight down as is shown in religious pictures.

The Hebrew University concluded that the legs were bent upwards at the knee and nailed on a level with the thighs; thus when the forelegs were broken the victim would be left hanging, thus accelerating death.

Of course we all understand what is meant by "the Cross of our Lord Jesus Christ", referring to His sacrificial and redeeming work at Calvary, but we are here speaking of the wooden instrument of execution. Nearer to the time of the Reformation the cross symbol was reckoned idolatrous, as may be seen from the following quotation from the foreword to *Pictures from Pilgrim's Progress* by C H Spurgeon, the introduction being written by his son Thomas Spurgeon: "Bunyan did not intend by this the symbol which is now so commonly had in reverence; he had no respect for such baubles and idolatries. He meant that a burdened soul finds no peace until it trusts in the atoning sacrifice of Jesus."

An inscription of great importance here also is a cast of the Siloam Inscription, the original of which is in the museum in Istanbul, as Palestine was under Turkish sovereignty when it was discovered.

The Siloam Inscription: In 1880 some schoolboys were playing in the water tunnel and pool of Siloam when one of them slipped and, putting his hand out to save himself, felt some carving on the wall of the tunnel at about water level. Dr Schick, the German architect, was informed and the matter investigated. "It was Professor Sayce who first deciphered the inscription by candle-light, sitting in mud and water for hours to accomplish his task" (*Archaeology and the Old Testament,* M F Unger). The inscription was later cut out and removed to Istanbul.

Thus was discovered the Siloam Inscription which records the successful conclusion of the project of bringing the water from the Gihon spring in the Kidron Valley outside the city wall, to the pool of Siloam inside the wall. The tunnel is called Hezekiah's Tunnel.

2 Kings 20 v 20 records, "And the rest of the acts of Hezekiah, and all his might, and how he made a pool, and a conduit, and brought water into the city, are they not written in the book of the chronicles of the kings of Judah?"

2 Chronicles 32 v 30 says, "This same Hezekiah also stopped the upper water course of Gihon, and brought it straight down to the west side of the city of David."

Verses 1—4 of the above chapter tell how Sennacherib came against the fenced cities of Judah, and when Hezekiah saw that the king of Assyria purposed to fight against Jerusalem, "he took counsel with his princes and his mighty men to stop the waters of the fountains which were without the city: and they did help him." Verse 4 says, "Why should the kings of Assyria come and find much water?"

The Siloam Inscription tells how the diggers started from either end and met underground "pick to pick", and that the water flowed from the spring into the pool, so not only did they meet but they also had the levels right.

Merrill F Unger in his book *Archaeology and the Old Testament* had this to say: "The great conduit of Hezekiah, 1777 feet long and hewn out of the solid rock, is one of the most amazing devices for water supply in the Biblical period . . . Workmen employing hand picks, operating in a zig-zag fashion from opposite sides and finally meeting in the middle, excavated a conduit that averages six feet in height and which constitutes a remarkable engineering feat."

The Siloam Inscription also has an important bearing on the science of palaeography, as it was written in the Old Hebrew script in use up to Hezekiah's time, which was also a significant point in the dating of the tunnel. Unger says (page 275): "But with material precariously sparse, especially before 700 BC, the palaeographic importance of the Siloam Inscription is quite obvious."

A good deal of change in the layout of the Museum is in progress and more is envisaged. It is very much to be hoped that the new scientific outlook does not result in the banishment from the public rooms of items such as the Siloam Inscription and the Mesha Stone casts, as has already happened to the casts of the stela recording the Law of Hammurabi.

The next items to engage our attention here are casts Nos 125207 and 125205, being casts of inscriptions from "The tomb in the side of the rock".

Only the last four letters of the name of this inscription are decipherable, but may be linked with Isaiah 22 vv 15–16: "Thus saith the Lord God of hosts, Go, get thee unto this treasurer, even unto Shebna, which is over the house, and say, What hast thou here? and whom hast thou here, that thou hast hewed thee out a sepulchre here, as he that heweth him out a sepulchre on high, and that graveth an habitation for himself in a rock?" It is most probable that this is indeed the tomb of Shebna, hewn in the rock and with an inscription engraved upon it.

The inscription is in the archaic Hebrew script close to the time of Hezekiah and opens with the words, "This is the sepulchre of . . . iahu who is over the house." "Iahu" are the last four letters of Shebna's name in the Hebrew and he is described in the very words of Isaiah as being "over the house".

In this corner of the Room of Writing is Cast No 362, a cast of the Mesha Stone already dealt with in a previous section.

The exhibits in the centre case at this end of the room are descriptive of the cuneiform writing. No 12451 is a fragment of a tablet prepared by a scribe but left unwritten. Nos 78262 and 78260 are examples of the reed stylus used to impress the clay.

Here also are some practice tablets. The teacher has written three entries from a vocabulary for the pupil to copy on the reverse of the tablet (Old Babylonian, 19th century BC).

In the left-hand end case is No K228, a tablet of Ashurbanipal, 669–627 BC. It tells of his campaigns in Egypt and reception of a friendly ambassador from the king of Lydia (c650 BC).

The other side of this case contains cuneiform tablets. One is a Kassite — Babylonian Dictionary of 442 BC. No K56 is a list of words or sentences relating to legal transactions, on the left written in Sumerian and on the right in Akkadian.

Here also are two mathematical tablets, one giving square roots and the other multiplication of 1 to 50 by 45 (7th century BC). No K4331 is a list of various fittings for different kinds of ships; this is of the 7th century BC from Nineveh.

The right-hand end of the case has fragments of scholastic literature from the royal Assyrian library at Nineveh, dealing with aspects of school life, organisation, curriculum, method of teaching and the character and mannerisms of teachers and students.

Wall Case No 1, across from the doorway from the casts of the inscriptions displayed upon the end wall, contains a display illustrating the development of the alphabet, and Wall Case No 2, a display illustrating the development of the cuneiform script.

Items of interest include No 33236, a tablet with its envelope, recording the sale of a plot of land. The envelope has a duplicate text with the seals of seven witnesses upon it. This tablet and "envelope" records the sale of a plot of land for two thirds of a shekel of silver, dated 1749 BC.

Behistun Inscription (see pages 126 and 127)

Sir Henry Rawlinson deciphering the cuneiform script with a cuneiform tablet on the left

This has a parallel in Jeremiah 32 vv 9–11. (Although this may refer to a scroll, the procedure is the same.) The contract was written on a tablet which was enclosed in a clay "envelope" and sealed, a copy or résumé of the original text being written on the outside and sealed. Jeremiah says, "So I took the evidence of the purchase, both that which was sealed . . . and that which was open." Tablet No 92997 is a tablet of the Persian period of 505 BC, the time of Daniel; it is a security for the rent of a house.

Wall Case No 3: "Decipherment". This case contains photographs of the Rock of Behistun which is on the road between Baghdad and Teheran. As the Rosetta Stone was to the Egyptian hieroglyphics, so the inscriptions here were a major factor in the decipherment of the cuneiform script.

The inscriptions at Behistun were carved in an inaccessible part of the cliff 500 feet above ground, with a sculpture showing Darius the great king of Persia receiving submission of his twelve enemies.

It is accompanied by a description of his achievement in three languages, Old Persian, Babylonian and Elamite, each written in a different form of cuneiform script.

Between 1837 and 1847, Col Sir Henry Rawlinson scaled the rock several times and with the help of natives obtained squeezes of the text. The Museum still has these squeezes in its collection.

Prior to this, a German scholar named Grotefund had succeeded in deciphering from various other inscriptions the names of Darius, Xerxes and Artaxerxes, and their title of King.

The Old Persian was assumed to be alphabetic in character as it had only 40 different signs; also the words were divided, thus offering the best chance of decipherment.

From other cognate sources the Old Persian was known, and Grotefund, by giving the known values to what he assumed to be names and titles, discovered the key to the decipherment of the cuneiform texts. However, he did not pursue the subject and it was many years before any progress was made. Although not the only one involved, to Sir Henry Rawlinson must go a large part of the honour of having been instrumental in deciphering the ancient cuneiform script.

Professor Sayce in his *Fresh Light from the Ancient Monuments*, speaking of the Assyrian cuneiform, says, "The study of Assyrian now reposes on as sure and certain a basis as

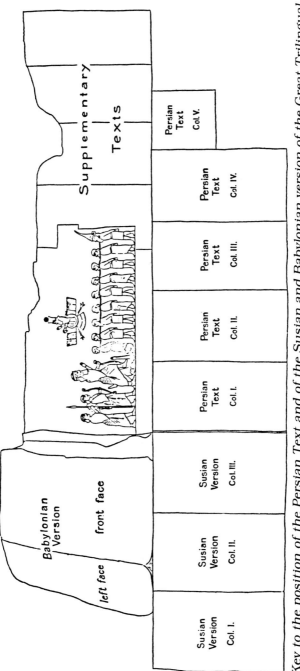

Key to the position of the Persian Text and of the Susian and Babylonian version of the Great Trilingual Inscription of Darius at Behistun

the study of any ancient language a knowledge of which has traditionally been handed down to us; and the antiquity of its monuments, the copiousness of its vocabulary, the perfection of its grammar, and the syllabic character of the writing — which expresses vowels as well as consonants — all combine to make it of the highest importance for the study of the Semitic languages. Its recovery has not only shed a flood of light on the history and antiquities of the Old Testament; it has served to illustrate and explain the language of the Old Testament as well."

Item No 88339 is a fragment of an alabaster vase inscribed with the name of Xerxes, king of Persia, written in four types of writing, Old Persian, Elamite, Babylonian in cuneiform and Egyptian in hieroglyphics.

Xerxes is the Ahasuerus of the Book of Esther; he reigned from 486 to 465 BC. The Book of Esther begins with the words, "Now it came to pass in the days of Ahasuerus (this is Ahasuerus which reigned, from India even to Ethiopia, over an hundred and seven and twenty provinces:) . . . In the third year of his reign, he made a feast . . .", so the story of Esther begins in 483 BC.

The Megillah or Scroll of Esther is of much interest. It was the last of the books taken in to the Canon of the Old Testament. Historically it represents the last period of the Old Testament; it has a place within the period of Ezra-Nehemiah.

One reason for its late acceptance was ostensibly that the name of God is not mentioned in it. However, in acrostic the divine tetragrammaton appears four times and the I Am once. Here God was working in a hidden way to preserve the earthly Israel, so His name is hidden. Information on this matter may be obtained from *The Companion Bible*, Samuel Bagster and Sons Ltd, or supremely, if access to the book is available, *The Introduction to the Massoretico-Critical Text of the Hebrew Bible* by Dr Christian Ginsburg.

The Scroll of Esther is traditionally read at the Feast of Purim which celebrates the deliverance of the Jews in the Babylonian last month of the year, Adar, which is about our March.

How amazing that such a small fragment as this piece of alabaster can bring to our minds such dramatic events

128

recorded in the history of the Children of Israel, from whom "after the flesh Christ came".

Item No 91033 is an octagonal prism of Tiglath-Pileser, king of Assyria. The writing on the prism was used by the Royal Asiatic Society in 1857 as a test for the decipherment of the cuneiform script. Col Rawlinson and three others separately translated it, the results being sufficiently alike to deem that the system of decipherment had been scientifically established.

The text describes the Assyrian campaigns against the Old Testament Meshech, mentioned in Ezekiel 38 v 3 and other places, the conquest of Carchemish, his hunting expeditions and building activities in Asher and other cities, and repairs to temples.

In the mid section of this case is a tablet with envelope (No 131449). This records a legal case concerning the division of the property of Hammurabi between Abba'11, king of Aleppo, and his sister Bittati, c1700 BC. No 17609 is an undertaking to repay after harvest, a loan of a homer of barley, and to shear a sheep for him, a rather fascinating form of interest (c1650 BC). This was a common form of contract now called harvest loans, in which the borrower promises to repay at harvest-time with interest. The names of the witnesses would be appended.

No 29793 is from the same writer to Amenophis III of Egypt giving greetings to the writer's daughter, one of the Pharaoh's wives. He has sent a statue of the goddess Ishtar of Nineveh and requests its return. No 29791 is from the same writer to Amenophis III and amongst other demands is a request for a gift in return for his daughter, whom Amenophis has married.

Here also is a photograph of Sir Henry Rawlinson and his notebooks showing transcription and study of the Behistun Inscription (mid and below). Looking at these notebooks gives us some idea of the meticulous and painstaking work which went into the decipherment of cuneiform script.

On Item No 113259, in the bottom left corner, is a mention of the mana, "a total of 100 manas of silver" lent to traders; this is of the time of Abraham, 20th century BC.

Wall Case No 4: "Historical Texts". In the upper section is the detail of a relief of Tiglath-Pileser III, king of Assyria, 745–727 BC, who is mentioned in 2 Kings 15 v 29 and five other times in the Books of Kings and Chronicles. This relief shows two scribes; one writes in cuneiform with a stylus on a clay tablet, the other writes in Aramaic with a pen on a parchment scroll.

Here also is the celebrated Taylor Prism from Nineveh, previously mentioned in the section on Assyria, and dealt with there.

The Assyrian records have a remarkable confirmation of 2 Kings 19 vv 36–37, where it is recorded that Sennacherib was slain by his sons Adrammelech and Sharezer in Nineveh. The records even give the date of the event as being on the 20th of Tebet, or December, 681 BC.

The Taylor Prism also records the defeat of Merodach-Baladan, king of Babylonia, the siege of Jerusalem and the tribute of Hezekiah, but does not mention the disastrous event which the Bible records, which was the cause of Sennacherib abandoning the campaign and returning to Nineveh without ever entering the city (2 Kings 19 v 35).

Merrill F Unger in *The Archaeology of the Old Testament* says, "It is generally agreed that the inscription of Sennacherib, though differing from the Biblical account in some particulars, really confirms it at virtually every point."

Continuing in Wall Case No 4, in the mid-section, is Item No K3751. This records the history of the first 17 years of Tiglath-Pileser III, king of Assyria, recording conquests and tribute. Amongst those bringing tribute is Jehoahaz (or Ahaz), king of Judah, 2 Kings 16 vv 7–9.

This is a very good example of one of the evidences that the divine tetragrammaton was pronounced "JEHOVAH". At one period an attempt was made by scribes to shorten all names beginning "JEHO" as it was too near the pronunciation of the Ineffable Name. Thus Jehoshua became Joshua, and there are many other examples (see Christian Ginsburg).

No K4401a records the history of the conflicts and alliances between Assyria and Babylonia from 1600 to 800 BC. This was drawn up to settle a dispute concerning the boundaries of the two kingdoms in the reign of Ashurbanipal, the "great and noble Asnapper" of the Bible.

Item No 92502 is a Babylonian chronicle listing the principal events which took place in Babylonia and Assyria between 744 and 669 BC, including the account of the murder of Sennacherib by his sons.

Wall Case No 4, lower section. Item No 22505 is a hexagonal prism chronicling the expeditions of Sargon II, king of Assyria,

Taylor Prism: Hexagonal clay prism inscribed with the details of eight campaigns by Sennacherib, King of Assyria (705–681 B.C.) Photograph: BM

Foundation Cylinder of Nabonidus mentioning his eldest son Belshazzar (550 B.C.) (see page 139)

721–705 BC, against Babylonia, Media, Syria and Palestine. Mention is made of his victory over Egypt and conquest of Samaria in 721 BC. In Isaiah 20, Sargon is mentioned and his victory over the Egyptians foretold.

Item No 35382 is a portion of a clay tablet inscribed with the annals of the reign of Nabonidus, king of Babylon. It records the defeat of Astyages, king of Media, by Cyrus, the capture and spoiling of Ecbatana his capital city, the taking of Babylon and the downfall and death of Nabonidus.

In the lower part of this case is also a copy of a treatise of Esarhaddon, king of Babylonia. In May 672 BC, Esarhaddon summoned his vassals to hear the proclamation of Ashurbanipal as crown prince of Assyria, and Samas-Sum-Ukin as crown prince of Babylonia. Originally there were eight copies made of this edict.

No 21901 is a Babylonian chronicle of 616–609 BC. This is of poignant interest as it includes a description of the fall of Nineveh in 612 BC to the combined attack of the Babylonians, Medes and Scythians. The fall of Nineveh was foretold by the prophets Nahum and Zephaniah. On the great wall sculptures in the saloons downstairs we saw the evidences of the fulfilment of their prophecies.

Item No 21946 is another Babylonian chronicle for the years 605–595 BC. It includes an account of the battle of Carchemish and the accession of Nebuchadnezzar II in 605 BC.

A passage tells of his capture of Jerusalem in 597 BC. In his seventh year in the month of Kislev, the king of Babylon mustered his army and marched to Palestine where he besieged the city of Judah. On the second day of Adar (16th March) he captured the city and seized the king (Jehoiachin), 2 Kings 24 vv 10–12. He appointed there a king of his own choice, v 17 (Zedekiah), received heavy tribute and brought it back to Babylon, 2 Kings 24 v 13. This tablet is from Babylonia.

Wall Case No 5: "Religion". No 93014 is a Babylonian-Sumerian bi-lingual account of the creation. Nos 93016 and 93017 are also creation tablets. Upon the decipherment of these tablets, "critics" of the Bible assumed that the Biblical account of creation was copied from the earlier Babylonian story. These accounts certainly came from a common source, but one corrupted and one preserved in purity. This being so, there are similarities, Professor Sayce says: "But with all the similarity, there is even greater dissimilarity. The philosophical conceptions with which the Assyrian account opens, and the polytheistic colouring which we find in it further on, have no parallel in the Book of Genesis. The spirit of the two narratives is essentially different" (*Fresh Light from the Ancient Monuments*).

Many years later, Merrill F Unger has written: "In the greatest possible contrast to the confusion and contradiction of these polytheistic narratives, the Genesis account, with chaste beauty and simplicity, which are eloquent evidence of its divine inspiration, presents the one eternal God as Creator and Sustainer of all things." Further, "The similarities on the whole are not particularly striking . . . The differences are, in fact, much more important. Their common elements point to a time when the human race occupied a common base and held a common faith. Their likenesses are due to a common inheritance, each race of men handing on from age to age records, oral and written, of the primeval history of the human race. The Biblical narrative, we may conclude, represents the original form these traditions must have assumed" (*Archaeology and the Old Testament*).

Next to the creation tablets is a Babylonian account of the Flood, No K3375, which is an 11 inch tablet of the Epic of Gilgamesh. No 231 is also the Epic of Gilgamesh.

Professor Sayce writes: "The Babylonians were well aware that the Deluge had been caused by the wickedness of the human race . . . Traditions of a universal or partial deluge are found all over the world; it is only in the Old Testament that the cause assigned is a moral one. The Chaldean account offers an exception to this rule."

Merrill F Unger comments on the resemblances between the Genesis and the Babylonian accounts as follows: "Both accounts hold that the Deluge was divinely planned. Both accounts agree that the impending catastrophe was divinely revealed to the hero of the Deluge. Both accounts connect the Deluge with the defection of the human race, although in the Epic of Gilgamesh the moral element is so blurred that, at first sight, one might conclude that the cataclysm was dictated by mere caprice. Both accounts tell of the deliverance of the hero and his family. Both accounts assert that the hero of the Deluge was divinely instructed to build a huge boat to preserve life. Both accounts indicate the physical causes of the Flood.

Both accounts specify the duration of the Flood. Both accounts name the landing place of the boat. Both accounts allude to the bestowment of special blessings upon the hero after the disaster."

The differences are listed as follows: "The two accounts are in diametrical contrast in their theological conceptions. Their idea of deity is completely divergent. This is the basic consideration that places the two stories poles apart. The two accounts are in diametrical contrast in their moral conceptions . . . The Babylonian flood stories are of very doubtful ethical and didactic value. The Biblical account . . . is of the highest didactic and spiritual purpose . . . The two accounts are in diametrical contrast in their philosophical conceptions.

"The correct explanation of the genetic affiliations between the two accounts seems clearly to be that Hebrew and Babylonian accounts go back to a common source of fact which originated in an actual occurrence."

A further anecdote of the late Rev L T Pearson may fit in here. Leonard took some ancient bones which he had recovered from under the Flood silt at Kish to an expert in such matters. The expert said, "What are these?" Leonard replied, "Tell me what you think and I will tell you what I know." The expert: "They are very ancient, probably 6000 years old." LTP: "You are right." Expert: "How do you know?" LTP: "Because they are of a man drowned in the Flood." Expert: "The Flood? What Flood?" LTP: "Noah's Flood." Expert: "Noah's Flood? Nobody believes in that nowadays." LTP: "This man did when it was too late."

We might ask ourselves, "Do I believe in the judgement of God upon sin, or will I leave it until it is too late?" "For the wages of sin is death; but the gift of God is eternal life through Jesus Christ our Lord" (Romans 6 v 23).

Finally, this case contains tablets with a prayer of Ashurnasirpal, the father of Shalmaneser III, to the goddess Ishtar.

Wall Case No 6: "Astronomy and Divination". Tablet No 86378 is a finely written tablet containing the first part of an astronomical treatise called "The Plough Star". It includes a list of the three divisions of the heavens, dates of the risings of the principal stars and those which rise and set together, and the constellations in the path of the moon.

"Mathematics", No 85194, is a collection of mathematical problems, some illustrated by diagrams. Solutions are required to a variety of problems concerning fortifications and siege works, water clocks, conical and cylindrical surfaces, cords of circles and areas of fields. In each case, the processes of solution and results are given.

The water clocks' formulae are of particular interest. These clocks were not time pieces but meters for measuring the volume of the flow of water, in the same way that a gas meter measures the flow of gas.

In the 1920's an American firm who were in association with an engineering firm at Redhill, Surrey, did an experiment using modern materials and the Babylonian formula to reproduce a "water clock". Their verdict was that they were not able to attain the degree of accuracy obtained by the Babylonians. Information as to how they knew this cannot be given. The engineers at Redhill were contacted, but their principal who would have known about it was very ill and could not answer letters before he died. The firm in the USA was written to but was no longer in existence. The facts as stated above were given to the writer by a friend who was with the Redhill firm at the time.

Wall Case No 7: "Administration and Law". Here is a representation of Hammurabi (Amraphel), king of Babylon, receiving the laws of the land from the enthroned sun-god, Samas.

At Susa, the Shushan of the Book of Esther, in 1901–2 was discovered a slab of black diorite over seven feet tall and about six feet wide, with engraved upon it almost three hundred paragraphs of legal provisions dealing with all aspects of Babylonian life. At the top of the stela the king is shown receiving the laws from the sun-god Samas, as we see in this case. At one time a cast of this stela was on display in the Museum, but this has now been removed. The original is in the Museum of the Louvre in Paris.

This Law of Hammurabi is of about 1700 BC, but since the finding of this stela, even older law codes have been found, one of about 1875 BC and another from an ancient city north-east of the modern Baghdad of an even earlier date. The discovery of these codes of law completely shattered the critical view that "detailed codes of law like those found in the Pentateuch are anachronistic for so early a period" (Unger). Here again is another example of how disastrously false critical opinion which rejects the Bible as the divinely inspired Word of God can be. These ideas are based on the theory of evolution, that man has gradually evolved in every area from a primitive base state to his present state of intellectual attainment. The evidence of Biblical archaeology proves this notion to be false.

Mrs Habershon says, "The fact that such a wise code should have existed in the time of Abraham has been urged as proof that the Mosaic Law was a copy of the Babylonian, but Genesis 26 v 5 makes it clear that God had already given a 'charge', 'commandments', 'statutes' and 'laws'." The verse reads, "Because that Abraham obeyed my voice, and kept my charge, my commandments, my statutes and my laws." Even from the earliest times God has made His will known, as may be seen in Genesis 4 v 7, which it is suggested could read, ". . . and if thou doest not well, a sin offering is at hand." Thus it may be seen that Hammurabi receiving his law from the sun-god is again a corruption of the real fact.

Before this Code of Hammurabi was found, the critics had been saying that the Book of Deuteronomy was written in the days of Josiah, and the other Books of Moses after that. This discovery undermined the very foundations of "the critical hypothesis". Instead of repenting of their error and folly the critics turned round and, with amazing effrontery, declared that the Mosaic Code was borrowed from Babylon. This Hammurabi discovery was one of many that led Professor Sayce, formerly amongst the critics, to declare that "the answer of archaeology to the theories of modern 'criticism' is complete; the Law preceded the Prophets, and did not follow them." But even this is not all; it is a canon of "criticism" with these men that no Biblical statement is ever to be accepted unless confirmed by some pagan authority. Genesis 14 was therefore dismissed as a fable on account of its naming Amraphel as a king of Babylon. "But," as has already been mentioned, "Amraphel is letter for letter the Hammurabi of the inscriptions."

A small item in this case, No K16026, is called the "Will of Sennacherib", whereby he gives his son Esarhaddon gold rings, necklaces, a diadem and other precious stones, the spoil of Bit-Amuki.

Wall Case No 8: "Letters and Nineveh Library". No 23145 is a letter from Hammurabi. No K114 is a letter to Sargon II, c 720 BC. No 23144 is another letter from Hammurabi. No K1352 is a partial catalogue of omen texts from the library of Ashurbanipal at Nineveh, and No K4375 is a type of dictionary.

In the lower section of this case are samples of El-Amarna tablets, formerly called the Tell el-Amarna tablets or letters. These tablets were found by a peasant woman in Egypt in 1887. She was given 10 cents for them by a dealer. Despite the efforts of the authorities, they were widely disseminated and 82 of them found their way to the British Museum. There were some 400 in all. These were translated by Col Conder. who said of them, "These letters are the most important historical records ever found in connection with the Bible . . . and most fully confirm the historical statements of the Book of Joshua, and prove the antiquity of civilisation in Syria and Palestine" (*The Tell el-Amarna Tablets* by C R Conder).

On the evidence of these letters, with their mention of the Habiru and appeals for help to Pharaoh from Palestine, Col Conder named Thutmose III as the Pharaoh of the oppression. One of the letters reads, "The Habiru plunder all the lands of the king. If archers are here this year, then the lands of the king, the lord, will remain; but if the archers are not here, then the lands of the king, my lord, are lost."

M F Unger says, "These invaders called Habiru are etymologically actually equatable with the Hebrews and although many problems are involved and the best scholars are divided on the matter, the statement of J W Jack is still pertinent, especially in the light of plain statements and clear intimations of the Old Testament concerning the date of the Exodus: 'Who were these invaders of southern and central Palestine? . . . Who else could they be but the Hebrews of the Exodus, and have we not here the native version of their entry into the land?'"

Moreover the name of Japhia, one of the kings killed by Joshua, is mentioned in the letters (Joshua 10 v 3), and also, in all probability, that of Adonizedek and Jabin, king of Hazor (Joshua 11 v 1),

Wall Case No 9. In the top section of this case is a 10-sided prism of baked clay, recording the building of a palace for Ashurbanipal, king of Assyria. The account is prefaced by annals concerning the early years of his reign. The campaigns include those against Taharqua (Tirhakah of the Bible), wars

Ashurbanipal as Basket Bearer

against Elam and the sack of Susa, and military operations against his rebellious brother ending with the capture of Babylon in 648 BC.

No 91109 is a barrel cylinder of Nabonidus, king of Babylon 556–539 BC; it gives an account of his restoration of the temple of Sin at Haran, and also the rebuilding of the temple of the sun-god Samas at Sippar. In the course of this work he found an inscription of Naram-Sin, the founder of the temple, about 2250 BC.

No 90864 is a stone stela bearing a relief of Ashurbanipal represented as a basket-bearer at the rebuilding and adornment of Esagila, the temple of the god Marduk, where his twin brother Samas-Sum-Ukin was appointed ruler, so that the strong might not oppress the weak (Babylon 668 BC).

On the mid-section of this case is No 117823, a clay cone or nail. In his *Through the Lands of Babylonia* Leonard Pearson says, "Now look at these cones or nails; they are rather similar to our dedication stones and are found embedded in masonry with just the head visible (although often plastered over). Information, such as names, found on them is helpful in estimating the period of the building." This reminds us of Isaiah 22 v 23, where speaking of the Messiah, God says, "And I will fasten Him as a nail in a sure place," although in that verse a nail to hang things on is meant.

Item No 22502 is a cylinder with an account of the first two campaigns of Sennacherib, king of Assyria, against Marduk-Apal-Iddina (the Biblical Merodach-Baladan), king of Babylon, against the Medes and other Eastern foes. It concludes with a description of Sennacherib's building activities at Nineveh (702 BC). Merodach-Baladan is spoken of in Isaiah 39 vv 1–2.

In the bottom section of this case is a basalt memorial stone giving an account of the restoration of the walls and temples of Babylon by Esarhaddon, the son of Sennacherib.

No 91128 is of especial interest to us as it is a foundation cylinder marking the restoration of the temple of the moon-god at Ur by King Nabonidus, ending with a prayer for himself and his son Belshazzar (Ur 550 BC).

Mrs Habershon gives the text of this cylinder as follows: "And as for me, Nabonidus, the king of Babylon, protect thou me from sinning against thine exalted god-head, and grant thou me graciously a long life: and in the heart of Belshazzar, my first born son, the off-spring of my loins, set the fear of thine exalted god-head, so that he may commit no sin and that he may be satisfied with the fulness of life (BM Guide A, p195). "

"When the critics first framed their indictment of Daniel, Belshazzar appeared to be a myth. It was known that Nabonidus was the last king of Babylon and that he was absent when Cyrus captured the capital. The contradiction between history and Scripture was complete. But the since-deciphered inscriptions have disclosed that Belshazzar was eldest son and heir to Nabonidus, that he was regent during his father's absence, and that he was killed the night the Persian army entered the inner city." It has been mentioned previously that Belshazzar promised to make Daniel the "third ruler in the kingdom" as Belshazzar was only second. What a thrill it must have been to find the name of Belshazzar, thus confirming the historicity of the Book of Daniel.

Our final piece before leaving the Room of Writing is No 22463. This is a copy of an older tablet by Nabonidus.

Perhaps a biographical note regarding E A Wallis Budge, the representative of the British Museum in Egypt during the later years of the nineteenth century, would not come amiss here as it was he who bought the eighty-two Tell el-Amarna tablets for Britain.

Of Budge, John A Wilson writes, "Wallis Budge might have posed for a protrait of John Bull. Indeed rumour said that he was related to the highest British families. He had a sturdy and portly frame, and his round face carried just the raising of the eyebrows which denotes a haughty (sic) and independent character. He always went his own way, which fortunately coincided with the desires of the trustees of the British Museum.

"An admirer of him wrote, 'Probably no Egyptologist of his stature . . . enjoyed a worse reputation among his colleagues than did Budge . . .' The same British critic wrote, 'I think that it is beyond question that Wallis Budge did more than any other man to rouse in the ordinary reader of this country an interest in the language and writings of ancient Egypt.' A similar statement might be made about American readers" (*Signs and Wonders Upon Pharaoh*, John A Wilson, University of Chicago Press 1964, p88).

The story of Wallis Budge in Egypt puts fiction to shame, not least for hilarity and adventure, and his acquiring of the Tell el-Amarna tablets.

Chapter XI
ANCIENT IRAN

Leaving the Room of Writing and proceeding straight on, the Neo-Hittite landing is reached. Turning right across the Ancient Anatolian Room, the Room of Ancient Iran is reached.

In the centre of this room is a relief panel in glazed brick (British Museum No 132525), part of a frieze representing the Persian royal guard, from the **palace of Darius at Susa**, c500 BC. This is on loan from the Louvre Museum, Paris.

Susa was excavated during the years 1884-1886 by the French archaeologist Delacroix, and some of its remains were re-erected in Paris.

M F Unger says, "It is now well known from excavations that Shushan the palace (Esther 1 v 2) refers to the Acropolis of the Elamite city of Susa, on which site magnificent ruins remain of the splendour of the Persian kings. The French excavations uncovered **Xerxes' (Ahasuerus')** splendid royal residence covering two and a half acres. The finds at Susa from the period of Xerxes were so astonishing that the Louvre in Paris devoted two large rooms to the exhibition of these treasures. In fact there is no event described in the Old Testament whose structural surroundings can be so vividly and accurately restored from actual excavations as 'Shushan the palace'" (*Archaeology and the Old Testament*, p308).

The *Pictorial Biblical Encyclopedia*, pp293-294, says of the Book of Esther, "The remains of Persepolis, and even more those of Susa, also bear out the events related in this book. Inscriptions found distinguish between Susa the capital (the royal palace) and the city of Susa. Thus the book correctly places the banquet in 'Susa the capital' (Esther 1 v 2).

"Excavations in Susa and Persepolis have brought to light many pillars over which coloured awnings were stretched as described in Esther 1 v 6. In Susa, the city street 'in front of the king's gate' (Esther 4 v 6) has been uncovered, and also the harem which had an exit on to the gateway of the city. This confirms the accuracy of the description of Esther standing in the inner courtyard of the palace opposite the king's hall, while the king sat on his throne inside the palace facing its entrance (Esther 5 v 1). From the harem a corridor led to the inner vestibule of the palace. In this same inner vestibule, opposite the corridor leading to it from the harem, was the throne room, the king's hall of Esther 5 v 2. The description of the banqueting hall opening on the palace garden is also correct in detail (Esther 7 v 7)."

On the right-hand wall of this room are three carved reliefs from the palace of Darius at Persepolis and two from the actual audience hall of Ahasuerus at Shushan the palace. One of these shows a file of Susan guards.

Information regarding the Scroll of Esther is given in the section on the Room of Writing.

In Ezra 4 vv 23–24 we read how the work of re-building the temple at Jerusalem was stopped until the reign of Darius, king of Persia. (This was Darius II.) Chapter 6 records that after a request for an investigation, ". . . Darius the king made a decree, and seach was made in the house of the rolls . . . And there was found a record thus written . . ." confirming the decree of Cyrus to restore the temple treasures and to re-build the temple. "In Ecbatana, the ancient capital of Cyrus, a copy of this edict has been found. Darius confirmed his predecessor's order and even instructed Persian officials to assist in the reconstruction of the temple" (*Pictorial Biblical Encyclopedia*).

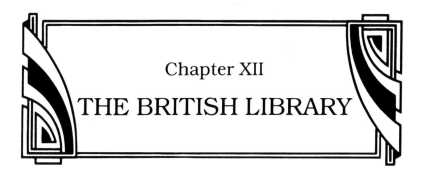

Chapter XII
THE BRITISH LIBRARY

Entering the Museum from Great Russell Street into the Entrance Hall and turning right, under the clock, we enter the galleries of the British Library, now a separate division within the Museum.

The first room is the **Grenville Library**; this contains many examples of manuscript illumination. The cases to the right contain examples of Continental work and those to the left show examples of English Illumination. The Continental work appears to be more sophisticated and delicately wrought than the robust English style; in both traditions the work and the fine colouring are remarkable. The examples of Early English Illumination are mostly Psalters.

In Case 1 on the left is the Vespasian Psalter, a Psalter in Latin, written and illuminated in Canterbury, probably at St Augustine's Abbey, during the second half of the eighth century AD. The inter-linear translation into Anglo-Saxon, added in the ninth century, is the earliest known copy of the Psalms in English (Cotton Ms Vespasian A 1 ff 3/0/b - 31).

Also here are the Four Gospels in Latin from Canterbury, of the same date.

Case No 7 contains the Luttrell Psalter in Latin, written and illuminated before 1340 AD for Sir Geoffrey Luttrell of Irnham in Lincolnshire. This manuscript is celebrated as one of the richest sources for scenes illustrating everyday life in medieval England.

Moving on, we pass into the **Manuscript Saloon.** Leaving the first cases which contain mainly literary autographs and music, we are confronted in Cases Nos 1 and 2 with the **Magna Carta**. The manuscripts shown in these cases trace the development of Magna Carta, the Englishman's chief bastion

Codex Sinaiticus

against arbitrary and unjust rule, although it must be said that it did not apply to all in the thirteenth century.

Manuscript No 1 in Case 1, is the Bull, so called from the Bulla or Seal attached, by which **Pope Innocent III** accepted King John's final grant of his kingdoms of England and Ireland to the Roman Church. This Bull, from St Peter's in Rome, dated 21st April 1214, recites the letters that John had sealed with a golden seal at St Paul's Cathedral in London on the 3rd October 1213, confirming the act of surrender and his promise to pay an annual tribute to the Holy See of 1000 Marks (about £666) — 700 Marks for England and 300 Marks for Ireland. The Pope's Bulla is appended at the foot by a silk cord (Cotton Charter VIII 24).

Articles of the Barons sealed by **King John** at Runnymede on the Thames in 1215:

The Manuscript No 2 in Showcase 1 contains the draft of the agreement made between King John and the Barons who had rebelled against him. This draft was expanded into the form of a charter and copies sent throughout the kingdom a few days later; two of the four surviving copies are shown as Nos 3 and 4 in the case.

After John's death the text was revised and re-issued three times by **Henry III**. The last revision, made in 1225, passed into the English Statutes as MAGNA CARTA, No 6 in the case.

Item No 4 in Floor Case 2 is a second exemplification of Magna Carta of 1215. Item No 5 is the Bull issued by Pope Innocent III condemning and annulling Magna Carta, in answer to representations made to him by King John. As a result of this, civil war broke out in England and continued until after John's death in October 1216. The Bull is dated AD 24th August 1216 (Cotton Ms Cleopatra El ff 155–156).

Item No 6 is an exemplification of Henry III's re-issue of Magna Carta dated 11th February 1225. There were three revisions and re-issues of Magna Carta during Henry's reign. The copy shown here was obtained by the County of Wiltshire and deposited at Lacock Abbey (Add Ms 46144).

Other floor cases contain chronicles of England, the death warrant of the **Earl of Essex**, maps and views, examples of modern calligraphy and a Nelson memorandum.

Moving on, we come to a case containing the **Sinaiticus and Alexandrian Manuscripts**. Reckoned to be the two most important Biblical manuscripts in the Museum, the Codex

Alexandrinus is designated "A" and the Sinaiticus by the first letter of the Hebrew Alphabet, "Aleph". The Alexandrian and Sinai Codices are fourth and fifth century examples of Bibles, with some parts missing and containing various Apocryphal books as was usual in pre-Reformation Bibles, on very fine quality vellum, which may be called Royal. It would seem that there is probably not much difference in the age of these manuscripts as the Sinaiticus has been dated to the late fourth century or even early fifth century AD.

Centre Cases Nos 1 and 2 contain more examples of **English manuscripts**; No 8 is the Floreffe Bible in Latin.

Another manuscript here in a centre case is that of the Lindisfarne Gospels, written and illuminated about 698 AD in honour of **St Cuthbert**, Bishop of Lindisfarne, who died in 687 AD. This is a masterpiece of book production and a historic and artistic document of the first rank.

Executed in the Monastery of Lindisfarne on Holy Island off the coast of Northumberland, it has an Anglo-Saxon translation inserted between the lines of the Latin text, a gloss of 950–970 AD (Cotton Ms Nero D IV).

In Bibles Case 1 is a Gospel of Thomas, a non-canonical book on papyrus in Greek, not later than 150 AD. This fragment, Papyrus 1531 Verso, was written in the third century AD.

Papyrus 2052 contains part of Genesis 5 and 6 in the old Latin Version, ie the Latin translation current before St Jerome. It is actually written on vellum. It was found at **Oxyrhynchus** in Egypt and is for half its length our sole authority for the text of the old Latin Version.

Egerton Papyrus 2 is a fragment of an otherwise unknown Gospel and is the earliest manuscript of Christian literature known to exist. It can hardly be later than 100 AD. The text coincides with all the four Gospels, its relation with that of John being especially striking.

This manuscript must be for us one of the most important and encouraging of all, confirming, as it does, that before the end of the first century AD the Gospels as we know them were in existence. Albright is sure that all the Gospels were written at an early date and that the **Gospel of John** was the first and not the last, as is commonly assumed.

From antiquity books were written on rolls of either vellum or papyrus, the vellum, made from animal skin, being much more durable. We call them scrolls, but scrolls suggest an "illuminated scroll" which we hold up vertically to read. Ancient books in roll form were held horizontally. These scrolls were composed of separate leaves sewn together in the case of vellum, or stuck if in papyrus, to make a continuous strip, which for convenience could be rolled. In later times the separate leaves were sewn together to form a book; this form is called a codex.

The fifth century **Alexandrinus** was presented to **King Charles I** in 1627 by a Patriarch of Constantinople named Cyril Lucar. It was transferred to the Museum by **King George II** in 1757. In many passages in the four Gospels affected by early variant readings, this codex gives support to the Byzantine text on which our Authorised Version is based.

The **Codex Sinaiticus** was discovered by a German scholar named **Tischendorf** among waste material which was apparently being used for lighting fires in the Monastery of St Catherine on Mount Sinai in 1844. Tischendorf made a second visit in 1859 when he added to his original find. The codex was presented to the Czar of Russia by the monastery in return for certain favours and decorations. After the Revolution it came into the hands of the Soviet Government from whom it was purchased by public subscription for the British Museum in 1933 for the sum of £100,000.

As the Codex Sinaiticus is contemplated the whole question of the modern versions of the Bible comes up before us, for it was upon this codex and the Codex Vaticanus that the Revised New Testament of 1881 was based.

The main influence on the Revision Committee was exerted by the Cambridge scholars **Westcott** and **Hort**. They exalted these two manuscripts to an unwarranted position of authority and their view has been widely accepted. They produced theories, some of which have been proved false by later investigations. However, the damage was done and the door opened to the flood of modern versions with which we are now familiar.

Sir Frederick Kenyon in his book *The Story of the Bible* says, "It might have looked, and indeed did look in 1881, as though the end of a period had been reached; it looked as if nothing now remained to be done . . .", so complete seemed the triumph of Westcott and Hort with the Sinaiticus and Vaticanus to accomplish Hort's stated aim, "to destroy that vile

Textus Receptus", the text underlying our English Bible of 1611. Quite soon, however, it became clear that some of the theories which they postulated rested upon insecure foundations.

Speaking of the Codex Sinaiticus in his book *The Revision Revised*, Dean Burgon says, "Next to Codex 'D' (Codex Bezae) the most untrustworthy codex is Aleph, the Sinaiticus, which bears on its front a memorable note of the evil repute under which it has always laboured; viz, it is found that at least ten revisers between the fourth and twelfth centuries busied themselves with the task of correcting its many and extraordinary perversions of Scripture."

In his Bampton lectures on the Divinity of our Lord, delivered in 1866, Canon Liddon gave a timely and solemn warning of the perils which then beset the church of Christ through the denial of our Saviour's essential and eternal deity. The detractors of this vital truth of God's Word have found a powerful ally in the modern versions which have been based upon the pro-Arian type of Greek text exhibited by manuscripts of the Vatican/Sinai group. Perhaps the most powerful unitarian assailants of the true doctrine of Holy Scripture today are the Jehovah's Witnesses. It is significant that their own version follows this type of text and that they are generally disposed to welcome versions like the Revised Standard Version and New English Bible, which display similar deficiencies and rest upon the same unsound foundation.

The above quotation is from a tractate entitled "The Providential Preservation of the Greek Text of the New Testament" by Ergatees, published about 25 years ago, since when the number of modern versions has increased.

Charles D Alexander, commenting on 1 John 2 vv 22–23 says, "To deny the Son is to deny the Father, and by consequence to deny the Incarnation of God, to deny the Holy Trinity and dismantle the Godhead. In these last days we are seeing this spirit of antichrist coming to its full and final blasphemy — helped on its way by the multiplicity of 'Bible' versions by which the Church is troubled, for most if not all the new 'versions' omit or otherwise meddle with the key texts on which the doctrine of God in Three Persons is founded."

Bibles Case 2: In this case is a copy of the Pentateuch and the Book of Joshua paraphrased in Anglo-Saxon by **Aelfric the Grammarian**, Abbot successively of Cerne and Eynsham. This is of the eleventh century AD, and is illustrated with coloured drawings (Cotton Ms Claudius B IV ff 50b–51).

Bibles Case 3: This contains Bibles in English, French and Latin and a Psalter in Latin.

Bibles Case 4: Here is a Psalter in Latin and a Gospel book in Latin as well as the Four Gospels of **Tzar Ivan Alexander** of Bulgaria written in the Slavonic of Bulgaria 1331–1371 AD. It contains 366 illustrations to the Gospels, and family portraits. Saved from the Ottoman Turks in 1393, it was finally taken to the Monastery of St Paul on Mount Athos. There it was discovered by Robert Curzon in 1837 and presented to him as a souvenir of his visit (Add Ms 39627 ff 2b–3).

Historical Manuscript Cases 1–4: Near the entrance to the Department of Manuscripts are Cases 1–4, labelled "Historical Documents". The manuscripts, shown in chronological order, start at the end of Case 1 farthest away from the entrance to the Manuscript Saloon. It is well to note that Case 1 is backed by Case 4, and Case 2 by Case 3.

Case 1: The first manuscript in Case 1 is from the Remembrances (or Memoranda) of **Thomas Cromwell**, made to aid his work as chief minister and Principal Secretary to Henry VIII. The page shown dates from late 1533 or early 1534, after the king's secret marriage to Anne Boleyn and the birth of the future Elizabeth I.

Catherine of Aragon had been deprived of her title as Queen, and was to be known as Princess Dowager, for she was considered only as the widow of Henry's brother Arthur, to whom she was originally married. The declaration in England that her marriage to Henry was invalid set the scene for the breach with Rome; although it must be said that the first move in breaking away from the domination of Rome was Magna Carta. The Act of Succession passed by Parliament early in 1534 recognised the new dynasty and the rights of its offspring (Cotton Ms Titus B1 f 462).

Cotton Ms Cleopatra EV f 327 — **The Six Articles** of 1539: The Act of the Six Articles established the conservative nature of Henry VIII's church settlement. The king had taken great interest in the debates between the Bishops in the House of Lords, which preceded the drawing up of the articles, and the draft is corrected in his own hand. In the preamble, shown here, he added that he was supreme head of the Church "by Godes law".

Harley Manuscript 6986 f 23 is a letter from **Princess Elizabeth** to her half-brother **Edward VI**. Elizabeth spent much of her early childhood with her brother Edward. Difficulties and suspicions arose once Edward became king.

After the fall of the Lord Protector, Somerset, power passed to John Dudley, Duke of Northumberland, whose policy was to prevent all contact between the king and his sister. The short-lived triumph of this policy was the setting of the crown on the head of his daughter-in-law, **Lady Jane Grey**, when Edward died.

It is clear from this letter that Elizabeth attempted to see Edward, perhaps during his final illness in 1553, but had been turned away.

The next item is a page from the diary of Edward VI, the boy king, son of Henry VIII and **Jane Seymour** and half-brother to Elizabeth. He was favourable to the Reformation, having been instructed in the doctrines of Scripture, but was weak in body and died in 1553 at the age of 26.

Henry VIII had decreed, by reason of a treaty with the king of Spain, that if Edward died without issue then **Mary Tudor**, daughter of Catherine of Aragon, should come to the throne, the next in succession after her to be the daughter of Anne Boleyn, Elizabeth; this in spite of the fact that Henry's marriage had been declared invalid because of her marriage to the king's brother.

Upon Mary's accession to the throne began the years of the Marian persecution, designed to stamp out the Reformation in England and to restore the supremacy of the Pope.

An old edition of *Foxe's Book of Martyrs* has a list of 315 names of those who, in the five years of Mary's reign, sealed their testimony with their blood; however, the editor states that owing to lack of space the names of many had to be omitted.

The list reveals a wide range of class and occupation including labourers, blind girls, a blind boy, a crippled boy, widows, tradesmen, gentlemen, ministers, Protestant priests, and the Bishops Ridley and Latimer and Thomas Cranmer, Archbishop of Canterbury. These all joined the great army of martyrs mostly being burned alive in public, some in groups of seven.

Before this time there were those who suffered for the Faith. The example of one, **John Fryth**, will suffice here. Fryth was one of the leading scholars in England; embracing the doctrines of the Reformation he fled to the Continent, where he worked with William Tyndale on his translation of the Bible into English. Because of his concern and love for the Protestant Christians in England, he felt that he must return to comfort and build them up. After many adventures he was finally captured and sentenced to death.

After sentence he was taken to Newgate and shut up in a dark cell, where he was bound with chains on the hands and feet as heavy as he could bear, and round his neck was a collar of iron which fastened him to a post so that he could neither stand upright nor sit down. His charity never failed him. A tailor's apprentice, twenty-four years of age, **Andrew Hewitt**, was placed in his cell. Fryth asked him for what cause he had been sent to prison and he replied, "The Bishops asked me what I thought of the sacrament and I answered, 'I think as Fryth does.' The Bishop of London said, 'Why, Fryth is a heretic and already condemned to be burned, and if you do not retract your opinion you shall be burned with him.' 'Very well,' I replied, 'I am content,' so they sent me here to be burned along with you."

On the 4th July 1533 Fryth and Hewitt were taken to Smithfield and fastened to the stake back to back; the torch was applied, the flame rose in the air, and Fryth stretching out his hands embraced it as if it were a dear friend whom he would welcome. Hewitt died first, and Fryth thanked God that the sufferings of his young brother were over. Committing his soul into the Lord's hands, he too expired. **William Tyndale** was himself captured on the Continent and strangled at the stake before being burned. Such was the cost of our English Bible. Some 95 per cent of the Authorised Version is Tyndale.

Mary, the daughter of Catherine of Aragon, married her cousin **Philip of Spain** in Winchester Cathedral on 25th July 1554. The match was not popular in England but her choice was influenced by her determination to bring the country back to Catholicism.

The Cotton manuscript Titus B ii f 100, shown here, is an order to the Justices of Norfolk dated 26th March 1555, and is signed by Philip and Mary as joint sovereigns. It orders the Justices "not only to aid and assist (Catholic) preachers sent into the country, but also to be present at the sermons and to use the preachers reverently; to 'travell soberly' with those who would not attend and conform, the wilful and more obstinate to rebuke and bind them over to 'good abearing' or to commit them to prison as the quality of their persons and circumstances may deserve."

A letter from the collection of **John Foxe**, the martyrologist, next claims our attention. It is a letter written in 1557 by **Thomas Bentham**, a Protestant minister of London, to Thomas Lever, minister to the congregation of English Protestant refugees in Aarau in Switzerland, and describes popular sympathy for seven Protestants burned at Smithfield the previous month. The victims had been arrested at a meeting held in a field outside the city; according to one account, Bentham spoke to the crown in their support. After Elizabeth's accession, he became Bishop of Lichfield (Harley Ms 416 f 63).

About Philip of Spain and Mary, John Foxe writes, "Regarding their expectation of the birth of a child. It was announced in Parliament that the queen was in an interesting situation, however both Mary and her husband were much disappointed by their illusory hopes and Philip seemed now less inclined to prolong his stay in this country. His doubts and difficulties were speedily solved by the astounding event which took him and the world by surprise, viz the abdication of his father, the emperor Charles V. Philip then left the kingdom, much to the grief and disappointment of the queen, nor does he figure again in our history until he sent his 'invincible **Armada**' against England in the reign of his sister-in-law Elizabeth."

On the 17th November 1558 Queen Mary died at the age of 43, having reigned for five years, four months and eleven days. Her half-sister **Elizabeth** succeeded her. "Elizabeth passed through London amid all the joys that a people delivered from the terrors of fire and slavery could express" (*Foxe's Book of Martyrs*, John Foxe).

Add Ms 35830 f 173 is a letter from the Scottish Reformer, **John Knox**, to Nicholas Throckmorton. Knox wrote the first part of "The Blast of the Trumpet Against the Monstrous Regiment of Women" in Geneva in 1558, prompted by the role played by Mary I and other women rulers in opposing the Reformation. He advocated the most stringent conditions when it was suggested that **Mary Queen of Scots** should return to England from France, where she had been queen consort of **Francis II** (died 1560). By the time this letter was written, on

6th August 1561, Mary's return had already been decided on and she arrived on the 19th August. At the same time Knox wrote a letter to Elizabeth complaining of Mary's attempts to prejudice his standing at the English court because of the book which he had written.

Something of the background of Knox's Scotland would seem appropriate here. "The Clergy had long been a by-word in Scotland, the butt of Court satire and of village horseplay. As were the people so was the Priest, as was the Noble so was the Bishop — indeed, what were Abbacies and Bishoprics but common perquisites for the cadets or illegitimate children of the nobility" (Lord Eustace Percy, *John Knox*). In time, however, the Bishops had taken control in the council of the land and their advent had been marked by the beginning of persecutions. **Patrick Hamilton** the proto-martyr had been burnt at St Andrew's in 1528.

When about 33 years of age, John Knox heard a preacher of the Reformed Religion named **George Wishart**. In 1525 Wishart had fled from Scotland on being accused of heresy for having taught the Greek Testament in the Grammar School at Montrose. After his flight from Scotland he preached in the West of England. When charged with heresy he had recanted and "burnt his faggot" at Bristol. Later Wishart was burnt at the stake in Scotland.

When heard by John Knox, Wishart had returned to Scotland steeled to a dangerous adventure. He was the first to bring to Scotland the word that had already changed Europe. True, he had forerunners, but in Wishart's mouth the word was no longer one of private devotion; it became a public proclamation.

"It was the proclamation not of a new theology, but of a new freedom. To him as to the fathers of the Reformation, the rediscovery of the New Testament had been quite literally a deliverance. 'Justification by faith' was an experience before it became a dogma. As the Middle Ages closed, a darkness settled upon Europe: upon the policy of Christendom, the darkness of pestilence, internecine war, Asiatic invasion and ecclesiastical schism; upon the soul of the individual Christian the darkness of a sense of guilt and failure. God's judgements were in the earth, and then in the darkness the simplest thing in the world happened — and the most incredible. Suddenly the prison door had swung on its hinges. 'I felt,' said Luther of his own experience, 'as if the doors had opened to me and I had entered into Paradise.'

"It was on the master text of the Reformation, Romans 8 v 1, that Wishart first preached in Dundee; it is difficult to imagine its effect on men, disillusioned with the world and themselves, who heard it for the first time in their own tongue. Here was no programme of liberation, but the conviction of freedom already won, the glorious liberty of the children of God.

"It was recognised that Knox had a remarkable gift of preaching and so he became a Protestant preacher. Looking back on this time he said, 'Not only those of the castle but also a great number in the town, openly professed by participation of the Lord's Table in the same purity that is now ministered in the churches of Scotland'" (Lord Eustace Percy, *John Knox*).

In 1546–7 some Protestant revolutionaries had established themselves in the castle of St Andrew's. To aid the Scottish authorities, a French fleet of twenty one war galleys arrived off St Andrew's, but were beaten off. Later reinforcements arrived from the Border, the castle was taken and John Knox with' it. He along with other captives were left in the ships as galley slaves, Knox remaining for nineteen months. In February or March 1549 he was released with the other captives. The king of France, Henry II, had a purpose in this leniency; he was playing for nothing less than a kingdom, and the hope was that these men, as future grateful subjects, might be of use to him. Later Knox became the focus for the fight for liberty and the main founder of the **Church of Scotland**.

The next item in Case 1 is a letter of Mary Queen of Scots to **Sir Francis Knollys**.

Mary Queen of Scots was sent to France as a child and was ultimately married to the Dauphin, who, following the untimely death of his father, became the king of France. He then laid claim to the Scottish crown and secretly to that of England also.

It was expected that **Francis II** would outlive Mary on account of her poor health, but he died on the night of 5th December 1560. Mary returned secretly to Scotland on 19th August 1561, where she assumed the role of queen for six years of intensely troubled reign. She was finally discredited and imprisoned at Loch Leven.

Mary escaped from Loch Leven in 1568 and fled to England. Her presence in England was a considerable embarrassment to

Elizabeth. She was a natural focus for discontent and plots against the Crown. After nearly twenty years she was brought to trial for complicity in the Babington Conspiracy and sentenced to death.

This is her first letter written in English to Sir Francis Knollys, who had the charge of her and taught her English (Cotton Ms Caligula C1 f 218).

The Execution of Mary Queen of Scots, 1587: Despite Elizabeth's indecision, Mary was executed in the hall of Fotheringhay Castle on the 8th February 1587. The drawing of the scene shown here comes from the papers of Robert Beale, Clerk of the Council, who carried the death warrant to Fotheringhay and read it aloud as a preliminary to the execution. John Knox had died some sixteen years before this on 24th November 1572 (Add Ms 48027).

Historical Documents Case No 2: The first item in Case No 2 is a letter of Queen Elizabeth I to **King James VI of Scotland** (James I of Great Britain) dated 18th May 1594. James was a troubled 27 and Elizabeth 61. The queen says that she was aware of the foolish foreign negotiations into which he had been tempted by his over-hasty desire to occupy her throne (Add Ms 23240 f 132b).

Drake's Treasure: Next after this letter is a Warrant to the Masters of the Jewel House and the Mint, dated 26th April 1584. It provides for the delivery of silver bullion to the **Earl of Leicester**, who had been an adventurer in the voyage of discovery attempted by **Sir Francis Drake**. This was Drake's voyage round the world in the Golden Hind, from which he returned in 1580 (Harley Ms 6986 f 37).

James to **Prince Henry:** Elizabeth died in the early hours of 24th March 1603. James had no time to see his eldest son Henry before leaving for London, where he had been immediately proclaimed King of England on the death of Elizabeth, and so wrote him this letter of advice (Harley Ms 6986 f 65).

Letter of George Villiers, **Duke of Buckingham**, and **Prince Charles** from Spain, 1623: On the death of Henry, Prince of Wales, in 1612, the hopes of Protestant England rested upon the succession of his younger brother Charles, but Charles came increasingly under the influence of the Duke of Buckingham, "Steenie", his father's favourite. Charles and Buckingham left the country secretly in 1623 to pursue the unpopular policy of alliance with Spain by negotiating a marriage between the Infanta and Charles. James was persuaded to support their embassy, but it ended in failure. The letter shown here is signed by both Charles and "Steenie". Charles concludes, "Your Majesty's humble and obedient son and servant"; Buckingham concludes, "Humble slave, servant and dog, Steenie" (Harley Ms 6987 f 48).

The Dissolution of Parliament, 1629: In this "news" letter Justinian Isham describes the stormy scenes in the Commons on the final day of the last Parliament before Charles I's period of personal rule. One of the members imprisoned after these events was Sir John Eliot, who died in the Tower and became the martyr of the Puritan Party (Harley Ms 383 f 82).

William Laud, Archbishop of Canterbury: For many, Laud was the embodiment of the autocratic power which Charles I attempted to exercise through his chief ministers, and of the wrong direction taken by the English Church under the influence of "High Church" or "Armenian" divines.

The discontented found refuge in Holland. The letter here is from Laud to the English Ambassador at the Hague, written on 24th May 1638. It shows that it was impossible to control emigration of Puritans to Holland, or the return to England of their opinions in the form of smuggled books (Add Ms 6394 f 291).

The next item here is a letter from **Oliver Cromwell** to Oliver St John in 1643. The letter is an appeal for funds to maintain the Parliamentary forces. Cromwell's experience at this time led to the formation of the New Model Army, which turned the tide of war the following year (Add Ms 5015 f 6).

Letter of Charles I to the Earl of Newcastle, 1642: The Civil War began when Charles I raised his standard at Nottingham on 22nd August 1642. He then moved his headquarters to Shrewsbury, from where he wrote to Newcastle, his commander in the north, this plea for the speedy raising of troops. Newcastle survived the war and was created Duke of Newcastle by Charles II in 1665 (Harley Ms 6988 f 125).

Cromwell at the Opening of Parliament, 1658: In 1657 Cromwell had refused the title of King and continued as Protector. On 20th January 1658 he opened the new session of Parliament. The next letter in this case describes the scene and was written by Thomas Fox MP on 23rd January 1658.

Cromwell died the following September (Stowe Ms 185 f 123).

Charles II to his "Friends" in England, 1659: Oliver Cromwell died on 3rd September 1658. Royalists became increasingly more open and other men's minds turned toward the restoration of the Monarch. Charles waited hopefully in Holland.

This letter was drafted by **Edward Hyde**, his most faithful adviser, virtual head of government in 1660, and created **Earl of Clarendon** in 1661. His "History of the Rebellion", the most important account of the Civil War, was written when he accompanied Charles into exile in 1646. In the letter Charles says that he intends to rule by and with the advice of "free and frequent Parliaments". One might wonder, on whose side was the rebellion, when it was caused by Charles I abandoning parliamentary rule and taking power into his own hands (Egerton Ms 2536 f 450).

Letter of Sir Philip Musgrave to Edward Nicholas, 1660: Edward Nicholas had been Secretary of State to Charles I and, although an old man, he briefly held the same office under Charles II. Sir Philip Musgrave was a staunch Royalist, as this letter shows. Ten of the twenty-nine people who passed sentence of death on Charles I or signed the death warrant were executed in 1660. Musgrave was appointed Governor of Carlisle. He and others like him did much to secure the loyalty of the provinces to the royalist settlement (Egerton Ms 2537 f 227).

General Monck and the Restoration: The army was the key to power in the final confused months of the interregnum. The remnant of the Long Parliament of 1640, the Rump, had been recalled in May 1659 in an attempt to find an indisputably lawful form of government. In October the army expelled the Rump, but the next swing of the pendulum had already begun. A group of army officers attempted to seize the Tower and wrote to Fleetwood, the Commander-in-Chief, justifying their action against "this strange new Parliament whose liberty and safety either of meeting or debating must be at your pleasure."

On the day that this letter was written, **George Monck**, Commander of the Army in Scotland, had called for a free Parliament. In January he marched south and in February entered London with his troops. The Rump was restored, paving the way for a general election and a Parliament which at once invited **Charles II** to return to his kingdom.

Monck was created Earl of Albermarle; the first signatory of this letter, Anthony Ashley Cooper, became one of the leading Whig politicians of the succeeding twenty years and **Earl of Shaftesbury** in 1672 (Sloane Ms 4165 f 48b). End of Case 2.

Historic Documents Case 3: The first letter at the top of Case 3 is a letter of Charles II to **Sir George Downing** in 1672. Sir George was sent to Holland with specific instructions to stir up discontent between Holland and England. Charles and **Louis XIV** of France had already made secret plans to provoke a war with the Dutch. Sir George returned to England on 7th February 1672, on the 17th March England declared war on Holland (Stowe Ms 142 ff 84b 85).

The next letter in the top line is from Richard Talbot, **Earl of Tyrconnel,** to King James' Secretary of State, Charles Middleton; James had appointed the Earl Viceroy of Ireland. The letter anxiously enquires about the sailing of the Dutch fleet for England bringing **William, Prince of Orange**. Tyrconnel eventually sent 3000 men but was unable to help James II's cause in England. This is another example of the continuing struggle between the Roman Catholics and the Protestants, the one to re-establish Roman Catholicism in the realm and the other to prevent it (Add Ms 41805 f 87).

The next letter below is a report to **John Grenville**, Earl of Bath, Lord Lieutenant of Devon and Governor of Plymouth, reporting the arrival of William of Orange at Torbay in 1688. The Dutch fleet slipped down the Channel aided by what was known for generations as the **"Protestant Wind"**. William was invited to take the crown with the object of establishing the Protestant faith in England (Egerton Ms 2621 f 73).

Other letters in this section concern **Queen Anne, George I** and the **Duke and Duchess of Marlborough.**

In the next section of Case No 3 are letters of **Sir Thomas Walpole, Captain Cook** and **George III** regarding the American War of Independence, a letter to **John Wilkes** who supported the Americans (and incidentally first suggested **British Summer Time**), another written by **Warren Hastings**, the first Governor General of India, and Nelson's last letter to Lady Hamilton.

These are followed by a letter from **William Pitt** to **Jeremy Bentham**, the social and prison reformer, and a letter from Charles James Fox, England's Foreign Minister, to **Talleyrand** of France in 1806 regarding negotiations concerning

Napoleon's conquests in Europe. These negotiations were not brought to a conclusion; England and Russia refused to recognise Napoleon's conquests. This was after the **Battle of Trafalgar** on 21st October 1805 had shattered Napoleon's ambitions to expand French influence overseas.

The final item in the bottom right-hand corner of the case is the notebook of **Dr Robert Willis**, Physician to **King George III**, concerning the illness with which the king was permanently afflicted from 1811 to his death in 1820 (Add Ms 41733H ff 18b 19).

Historic Documents Case No 4: The first item in Case No 4 is part of **Wellington**'s despatch after the **Battle of Waterloo** and is dated 19th June 1815, the day after the battle.

The despatch was addressed to the **Earl of Bathurst**, Principal Secretary of State for the War Department. A fair copy was made from this draft, which is in Wellington's hand, signed by the Duke at Brussels, and taken to London by Major the Hon Henry Percy who "laid it at the feet of **HRH The Prince Regent**".

The next item below is a memorandum made by **Sir Robert Peel** of the views of **William Wilberforce** regarding the abolition of the Slave Trade. The act was passed in Parliament by an overwhelming majority in February 1807 and Royal Assent was given on the 25th March. This act did not liberate the slaves, which only came to pass after the death of Wilberforce, but made the trade in slaves from Africa to the West Indies illegal. Wilberforce saw this as a first step to bettering the lot of the slaves, since if the supply ceased the plantation owners would then have to look after the labour which they already had.

William Wilberforce was born into a rich industrial family and was what we today would call a "playboy", a man about town. He came under the influence of the early Methodist preachers and also, later, of **John Newton**, the ex-slave-ship captain, when Newton was Vicar of St Mary Woolnoth, in London.

Wilberforce became one of the so-called **Clapham Sect**, a very influential group of Evangelical Christians who had houses facing Clapham Common. Under the influence of the First and Second Evangelical Revivals the face of England was changed, as may be learned from reading J Wesley Brady's *England Before Wesley and After*, and the country was saved from revolution such as happened in France. All this, the "English way of life", and the prosperity of the Western World, may be directly attributed to the release of the Greek New Testament beginning with Erasmus, finally resulting with the **Authorised Version of 1611**, and the **Protestant Reformation**.

Next to the Wilberforce document is a letter to **Francis Place**, whose efforts were largely responsible for the repeal against "combinations" of workmen, and laid the basis for modern **Trade Unions** (Add Ms 27803 f 299).

The item above this is a letter regarding **Napoleon** on St Helena, 1820 (Add Ms 15729 f 116b).

Next below is a letter from **Richard Cobden** dated 11th May 1836, highly commending **Roland Hill**'s ingenious plan for a penny post.

Above this is a letter of **Benjamin Disraeli** to his sister, dated 25th March 1838, describing preparations for **Queen Victoria's Coronation**, which took place three days later (Add Ms 37502 ff 82b–83).

Below are two letters of Queen Victoria (Add Ms 43049 f 233 and 43050 ff 155b 156).

Again above are two letters of **Florence Nightingale** from the Crimea, 1855 (Add Mss 43393 ff 161b 164b–165).

The letter below, and the last in this section of Case No 4, is a letter of 1861 from **Lord Palmerston** to **William Ewart Gladstone**. How relevant to our own time this letter is; Gladstone is objecting to increased naval expenditure. Palmerston's reply is that we must be stronger than a power which is likely "to make arrogant use of predominant power".

The first item at the top of the final section of Case No 4 is a letter from Gladstone to **Sir Henry Ponsonby**, Queen Victoria's Private Secretary, 1892 (Add Ms 45724 f 201).

The one below is the penultimate page of General Gordon's journal from Khartoum.

The reader may wonder, "What has **General Gordon** to do with the British Museum?" In the Manuscript Department are two of General Gordon's letters and the penultimate page of his journal, written from Khartoum shortly before his death, and later presented to the trustees of the Museum. Gordon was a man of the Bible, and on the statue of him erected in Trafalgar Square he is depicted with a Bible under one arm and the "wand of victory" under the other. Moreover his name is inseparably linked with the "place called Calvary", which he is erroneously thought to have named.

At Ashkelon, he recalled that "Napoleon I, Alexander the Great, Sennacherib, Nebuchadnezzar and a host of great men passed by this route." Titus came up by Gaza to Jerusalem and Richard Coeur de Lion was for years at Ashkelon.

The supposed sites of the holy places seem to have had peculiar fascination for him, and he came to the conclusion that most, if not all of them, were wrong.

During his stay in the Holy Land, from January to October 1883, Gordon would sometimes stay at Ein Kerem, the traditional birthplace of John the Baptist. From there he would visit the American family Spafford in their house on the North Wall of Jerusalem by the Damascus Gate. The house is still there in 1986, and in possession of the Spafford family. It is being used as a Children's Centre and Clinic for Mothers and Babies.

From 1872 to 1875 Lieutenant (later Colonel) **Claude Reignier Conder** RE surveyed the major part of the Holy Land, returning to England in September 1875, a full seven years before General Gordon arrived in Palestine.

We now turn to Col Conder's own words extracted from his book of 1878, *Tent Work in Palestine*, still some five years before Gordon arrived in Jerusalem.

"The 'place called Calvary' was according to our general idea the public place of execution. Some have supposed its name Golgotha or 'place of a skull' to be derived from this fact. We look naturally for some spot outside the city, and beside one of the great roads.

"The tomb could not have been one of the KOKIM tombs originally used by the Jews, in which each body lay in a long pigeon-hole with its feet towards a central chamber, for in that case angels could not have been seated 'one at the head and the other at the feet, where the body of Jesus had lain'. It must have been one of the later kinds of tombs in which the body lay in a rock sarcophagus under a rock arch parallel with the side of the chamber, closed by a rolling stone." It is important to note that this was written years before the discovery of the Garden Tomb.

To continue with Col Conder, "These considerations would lead us to fix Calvary, the place of execution, north of Jerusalem, near the main road to Shechem. Now close to this road is a rounded knoll with a precipice on the south side. This knoll is called by the natives, 'the Rent', being separated from the Bezetha Hill by a deep trench. Dr Chaplin tells me that the Jews still point out the knoll by the name Beth Has Sekilah, 'the **Place of Stoning**' (Domus Lapidationis), and state it to be the ancient place of public execution which is mentioned in the Mishnah, and which was apparently well-known at the time at which the tract Sanhedrin was written.

"The stony road comes out from the beautiful Damascus Gate and runs beside the yellow cliff. Above the cliff which is some thirty feet high, is the rounded knoll without any building on it, bare of trees, and in spring covered in part with scanty grass, while a great portion is occupied by a Moslem cemetery. The place is bare and dusty, surrounded by stony ground and heaps of rubbish, and exposed to the full glare of the summer sun. Such is the barren hillock which, by consent of Jewish and Christian tradition, is identified with the Place of Stoning, or of execution according to Jewish law."

There is much confirmation of this identification in the New Testament itself. According to W E Vine, the word used in all four Gospels for the place which is called "the Skull", is the Greek word KRANION, Latin CRANIUM, akin to Kara, the head. (The word used in the Authorised Version in Luke 23 v 33, "Calvary", is Latin and not the original Greek.)

The cranium is the top part of the head or skull which contains the brain, so that the description used of the place of execution means the summit, the head or top of the hill.

Mount Moriah was God's appointed place of sacrifice, but the temple area, the site of the old order of sacrifices, is not the summit of Moriah — Calvary is. The temple area is over 200 feet lower than the summit of Moriah. This place was reserved for the great anti-type of all the sacrifices, one of "nobler name, and richer blood than they".

W E Vine, in his *Expository Dictionary of New Testament Words*, says of Calvary, "The locality has been identified by the traces of the resemblance of the hill to a skull. This explanation has been widely accepted in our time, but it is entirely without foundation."

It has been stated that the rock has altered in appearance within living memory, so that it can be assumed with certainty that its appearance nearly 2000 years ago was not as it is now.

What then was General Gordon's part in all this? Stated simply, it was just that standing on the roof of Spafford's house and looking across to "the little green hill", he thought, "If this is Calvary there will be a tomb near." He set enquiries in motion which led to the discovery of the **Garden Tomb**, which exactly fills the requirements of the New Testament record. Far from discovering Calvary, General Gordon was the means of indisputably authenticating the **Hill of Calvary**.

There are many other evidences which could be adduced in support of the authority of this site, but the mention of two must suffice.

The first is the proximity of the wall at the time of the crucifixion. For long it was declared by the traditional school that the line of the present wall was the line of **Agrippa's Third Wall**. If this was the case, the Skull Hill could not be the place of Calvary, as the record says that it was "nigh to the city" (John 19 v 20).

In the 1920's **Professor Sukenik** definitely established the real line of the **Third Wall of Jerusalem**, running to the north of the present wall and enclosing the Hill of Calvary.

In 1936 **Hamilton**, excavating to the west of the **Damascus Gate**, found the foundation stones of the **Herodian Wall** in situ. This has been confirmed by **Professor Ehud Netzer** of the Hebrew University in recent times. In up to date Israeli publications the wall in the time of the Second Temple, which had not been destroyed in Christ's time on earth, is shown as coming along the line of the present North Wall. The maps still show the wall taking a right angle southerly turn, but it would not be unreasonable to say that this is conjecture as such a wall has never been authenticated. Claims have been made but nothing definite has emerged.

Another evidence, according to the Rev L T Pearson, is that when the foundations for **Mandelbaum House**, to the north of Calvary, were being excavated there were discovered "hundreds of tons of pure bone and wood ash". In Leviticus 16 v 27 we read, "And the bullock for the sin offering, and the goat for the sin offering, whose blood was brought in to make atonement in the holy place, shall one carry forth without the camp; and they shall burn in the fire their skins, and their flesh, and their dung." Here then was the "Place of the Ashes". If a line is taken from the north of the temple site to the Place of the Ashes, it will pass directly over the Hill of Calvary.

Perhaps the above account will enable any who are inclined to dissemble in this matter, to be assured, as Col Conder was, of the authenticity of this site.

The last thing that is desirable is that this site should become an object of veneration or worship. How thankful we should be that those who have control of the Garden Tomb see to it that this does not happen, but that it is made a place for the proclaiming of the Gospel of the redeeming Love of God in the supreme sacrifice of the Lord Jesus Christ in this very place.

Next to the page of Gordon's journal is Lenin's application for a British Museum Reader's Ticket.

His wife in her *Memories of Lenin* has written, "From the conspiratorial point of view things could not have been better. No identification documents were needed in London then, and one could register under any name. We assumed the name of Richter" (Add Ms 54579 f 2).

Above the Lenin document is a letter of **Sir Winston Churchill** of 1907 to **Campbell-Bannerman** (Add Ms 52516 ff 112b–113).

Below this is a letter of Robert Briffault from Flanders to his daughter describing the **Battle of Paschendale** in October 1917. His writings were of influence in the 1920's and 30's. This description was incorporated into his novel *Europe in Limbo* (Add Ms 58441 ff 60–61).

The next letter above is concerning **Neville Chamberlain**'s period of appeasement immediately preceding the Second World War. It is from Lord Cranbourne expressing his feelings on the subject to Paul Emrys Evans, a Conservative Back Bencher (Add Ms 58248 f 4b).

Below this is **Captain Scott**'s last polar journal made during the fatal expedition to the Pole in 1912 (Add Ms 51035 f 33).

The final item at the bottom of Case No 4 is a letter of **John Maynard Keynes**, the economist (Add Ms 57923 f 44).

In our journey through the Manuscript Saloon we have looked at some items of general interest, but mainly on records, perhaps not directly connected with the text of the Bible, which have given an insight into the background of our liberties of today, and into the cost in human terms of our English Bible with its New Testament based on the Greek of Erasmus, the Textus Receptus and Tyndale's translation into our language. It is no mere coincidence that the decline in morals and behaviour has coincided with the sustained attack on the authority, authenticity and historicity of our English Bible of 1611. The moral decline is spiritual at base, for when there is no final authority there is no norm of morality, and the situation deteriorates into that of the time of the Judges where "every man did that which was right in his own eyes" (Judges 21 v 25).

Chapter XIII

THE KING'S LIBRARY

Leaving the cases of Historic Documents and proceeding forward through the doorway in front of us, we enter the King's Library. This collection includes the library of **King George III** and was given to the nation by **King George IV**. The library was designed by Robert Smirke and constructed from 1823 to 1828. Not all the cases have items of interest to our subject, for here are displays devoted to such diverse characters as **Shakespeare** and **George Orwell**, and so we move around to those which are apposite.

In a case on the right as we enter is a display of **writing materials**. Amongst other examples are a Hebrew scroll on leather (OR 4221) and a parchment scroll of the Book of Esther (Add Ms 11831).

Broken pieces of pottery with writing on them are called Ostraca and here is an example inscribed in Greek. Ancient Hebrew examples have been found at Samaria and of particular importance, at Lachish, confirming the Biblical account of Sennacherib's advance on Jerusalem in the last days of Solomon's temple (Ostracon 14112).

Here also is a "book" of waxed tablets. These wooden tablets were coated in wax which could be inscribed with a stylus and smoothed over for using again. In Luke 1 v 63 we read that Zacharias, the father of John the Baptist, "asked for a writing table (tablet) and wrote saying, His name is John" (Add Ms 33270).

In the second section of this case is a page from a **Coptic Bible** written on papyrus from Upper Egypt. It shows the beginning of the Book of Deuteronomy (OR 7594 f 53).

A little further on are cases telling **"the story of writing"** with examples of writing from early times. The first item in

The Gutenberg Bible

Wycliffe's Bible

Case No 1 is a seal impression of property marks from Mesopotamia of about 3000 BC (WAA1930-12-13 423).

In the second half of this case are two examples of the **Cuneiform Script** on clay tablets. A brief description will suffice as such tablets have been considered in the Room of Writing.

(a) Is a tablet of about 3000 BC from near Kish in Mesopotamia. At Kish, Professor Woolley found evidence of the Flood (WAA 116625(1924-5-12)).

(b) Is an account of barley issued to workmen attached to various temples to pay other workmen — sub-contractors one would suppose. This tablet is from Gunu, Mesopotamia (Iraq), 2048 BC (WAA 1418 (96-4-6 16)).

In the second half of Case No 2 is an example of **Aramaic Script** written on papyrus from Egypt, 5th Century BC (Pap CV1 AB).

Aramaic was the common form of language in the Middle East in New Testament times, and that in which the Gospels would have been first recorded before being put into Greek as the gospel spread over the Greek world. There are several Aramaic words and phrases in our New Testament text.

A further case on the right is devoted to the earliest examples of printing from moveable type. Here are Bibles printed by **Johann Gutenburg**, credited with being the inventor of moveable type, one of the epoch-making events in world history.

The first in view is the Gutenburg 42 line to the page Bible. This Latin Bible, the first large scale use of moveable type, was the work of a partnership dissolved after the completion of the work — Johann Gutenburg, Johann Fust and Peter Schoeffer. Printed in Mainz 1455, 51 copies are known, 12 on vellum and 39 on paper. 20 are perfect.

Next to this in the case is an example of the 36 line Bible, probably printed by Gutenburg in 1458–9. This is a copy of the text of the **Vulgate** as used in the 42 line Bible.

On the side of this case are examples of the first European printing from moveable type; they are two **Letters of Indulgence**.

(a) The sixth issue of the 31 line indulgence, with 1455 given as the date of purchase (Anonymous Printer, Mainz, 1454–55).

(b) The fourth issue of the 30 line indulgence sold at Neuss on 29th April 1455 (Printer of the 42 line Bible, Mainz, 1454–55).

Priests travelled from town to town selling indulgences to raise money for various objects of the Roman Catholic Church. These indulgences were supposed to be for the forgiveness of the sins of the purchaser for a certain period, sometimes years. It is reported that in Rome itself the situation was so bad that forgiveness could be bought in advance for crimes intended to be committed.

It was this state of affairs which moved **Martin Luther** to nail his 95 theses to the church door at **Worms**. Luther had no intention of rebelling against the Pope. What he did was common practice by Professors of Theology to initiate public debate. Luther did not believe that the Pope would support such practices. At first the Pope did not take too much notice of the matter, but others realised the implications where he seemingly did not. The theses were taken up and rapidly spread over Christendom, since they involved the foundation of the Reformation, Justification by Faith, for "who can forgive sins, but God alone?" (Luke 5 v 21).

Wycliffe, Tyndale and **Coverdale:** Towards the end of the gallery are three cases of the English Bible. In the first section of Case No 1 is the first complete Bible in English. This is the John Wycliffe Version of c 1380–82 (Egerton Ms 617 f 165).

John Wycliffe was born in the early fourteenth century and has been called the "Morning Star of the Reformation". He anticipated Luther's attack on the practice of indulgences by some 150 years. He was Master of Balliol College, Oxford, and a Doctor of Divinity. For Wycliffe the Bible was God's Law to be understood and obeyed by all men, and made available to them "in that tongue in which they know best Christ's sentence". He condemned not only indulgences but also the doctrine of transubstantiation. This was the period when two Popes were struggling for the mastery, and Wycliffe was for a time unhindered. He set about his great work of translating the Latin Bible into English. Wycliffe's works were condemned as heretical in 1382, but he died in retirement two years later.

Wycliffe organised an order of poor priests called **Lollards** who travelled the country with portions of Scripture and tracts in English. These itinerant preachers were quite numerous and preached on village greens, in graveyards and sometimes even in churches, with great effect.

THE WALDENSES

In the valleys of Piedmont in North Italy the truths of Christianity were preserved by a pious and earnest people who clung to "the faith once delivered to the saints".

Space does not allow a complete description of this remarkable body of Christians, who clearly maintained the truth of Christianity among themselves during the Dark Ages when the Church was becoming more and more corrupt. They held to the truth of Scripture and refused all else as false. They had at least a large part of the Scriptures in their own tongue. An ancient author tells of one of their peasants who could repeat the whole Book of Job from memory, and of others who had the New Testament at their finger tips. Their piety was proverbial . . . their lives accorded with their profession.

The growth of this so-called heresy was viewed with alarm and they were pursued with the utmost violence. Lies and calumnies of the basest kind were spread regarding them. When the Inquisition was instituted in 1206 they were amongst the earliest objects of its activities. They were driven from their homes and treated with every cruelty the evil mind of man could contrive. Many were tortured, many burned alive. They were driven ruthlessly over the mountains to perish in the snows. Numbers took refuge in caves; fires were lit at the entrances and mothers with infants in their arms were stifled to death.

It was from the Waldenses that a Franciscan monk named **Raynard Lollard** received enlightenment. He, who had before been a persecutor, became a preacher of the gospel and finally suffered as a martyr, being burned at the stake at Cologne.

In spite of continued and violent persecution there were some 800,000 Waldenses in Europe at the time of the Reformation, which probably includes all who had such views.

Those in the South of France continued to suffer right up to the time of the French Revolution.

THE LOLLARDS

Thirty of these simple Christians came to England from Germany in the reign of Henry II (1154–1189). They were brought before a Council of Clergy at Oxford. Their spokesman said they were Christians who believed the doctrine of the Apostles and denied purgatory, prayers for the dead and the invocation of the Saints. The king, in conjunction with the council, ordered them to be branded with a hot iron on the forehead, to be whipped through Oxford, to have their clothes cut short by their girdles, and to be turned into the open fields, expressly forbidding anyone to succour them. It was the depth of winter and the whole company perished by cold and starvation. They died patient and serene repeating the Lord's words, "Blessed are they who are persecuted for righteousness' sake."

When Wycliffe died on 31st December 1384, the Lollards had become very numerous in England. The leaders of the Church determined to do their utmost to extirpate them.

The first martyr to die by fire in England was **William Sawtre**, a London clergyman. He was followed by a working man named **John Badby**, who also died in triumph, supported by divine grace.

Sir John Oldcastle, later **Lord Cobham**, used his wealth and influence to protect the Lollards. He circulated Wycliffe's works and maintained, at his own expense, many itinerant preachers. Wycliffe's books were publicly burned, including one which belonged to Lord Cobham. The king was appraised of this. Cobham was arrested and placed in the Tower. He was condemned as an "incorrigible, pernicious and detestable heretic". He escaped from the Tower and spent four years hiding in Wales. On his re-capture he was executed with shocking barbarity. He was hung in chains from the gallows over a slow fire and cruelly burned to death.

Shortly the London prisons were filled with the Lollards and their followers. It was decreed that they should be hanged on the king's account and burnt for God's. By a baptism of suffering, the way was prepared for a glorious reformation.

Tyndale saw that without the Bible it was impossible to establish the people in the truth. So he began his translation, from the **Greek of Erasmus**, in Little Sodbury, Gloucestershire.

To a priest sent to change his mind, Tyndale uttered his famous words, "If God spares my life, ere many years I will take care that a ploughboy shall know more of the Scriptures than you do."

He realised that he was on the point of being arrested and condemned, so fled to the Continent. After completing the New Testament he was finally betrayed, strangled and burned at the stake.

"Time (and space) would fail me to tell of those who through faith subdued kingdoms, wrought righteousness . . . were tortured, not accepting deliverance" (Hebrews 11 vv 32–40).

During the remainder of the reign of **Henry V** and right through the Wars of the Roses, confessors of the true Faith had no respite, whilst in the reigns of **Henry VII** and **VIII** the persecutions increased in bitterness. Neither age nor sex was spared. The Constitutions of Oxford forbade anyone to possess or read an English Bible without a bishop's licence. "Many true followers of Christ went to the stake and reached heaven through fire" (T W Carron, *The Christian Testimony Through the Ages*).

The copy of Wycliffe's Bible shown here belonged to **Thomas of Woodstock**, Duke of Gloucester, youngest son of Edward III.

In the middle section of this case is a copy of **William Caxton**'s Golden Legend, translated from the Latin and first printed in 1483, containing some portions of the Bible in English. The copy shown here was printed by Caxton's successor, Wynkyn de Worde, in 1498 (C 11 c f XLIX).

The next item is **William Tyndale's New Testament**, translated from the third edition of the Greek New Testament of Erasmus (1522), making reference to Luther's New Testament and the Vulgate.

At Oxford, Tyndale came into contact with the Greek New Testament of Erasmus; as he read, it "spoke to him of God, of Christ, and of regeneration" (*Reformation in England*, Banner of Truth, 1962). Because of opposition he moved to Cambridge, where he met with others who had been enlightened by the word of God. It has been said that from this group "the English Reformation began independently of Luther or Zwingli — deriving its origin from God alone" (*Reformation in England*).

Leaving Cambridge, he worked as a tutor to a family in Gloucestershire. Whilst here, Tyndale decided upon the major work of his life, the translation of the Bible into English, with the New Testament from the Greek.

In 1524, after failing to enlist the support of the Bishop of London for his project, he left England for Germany, first to Cologne, then fleeing to Worms, taking with him the sheets of the New Testament already printed. In Worms an edition of the New Testament was printed and was on sale in England by April 1526.

The English Bishops tried to destroy all the copies at home and abroad. His translation eliminated some familiar ecclesiastical words: he substituted "Congregation" for "Church", "Senior or Elder" for "Priest", and "Repentance" for "Penance"; these alterations were in accordance with the real meaning of the Greek words.

The ecclesiastical authorities sought to apprehend him and he was finally betrayed and captured in Antwerp, from whence he was imprisoned in the castle of **Vilvorde**, two leagues from Brussels.

After his arrest he continued his Old Testament translation in prison. It is highly probable that before his arrest Tyndale had completed his Old Testament translation to the end of Chronicles. At his death, he left in manuscript the books of Joshua to 2 Chronicles.

Tyndale was strangled at the stake and his body burnt on the 6th October 1536. His last words, proclaimed in a loud voice, were, "Lord, open the King of England's eyes."

In the third section of Case No 1 is **Coverdale's Bible** of 1535, the first complete Bible printed in English (G 12208).

Even as Tyndale died, the complete English Bible of his assistant, **Miles Coverdale**, based largely on Tyndale's work, was circulating in England. Two years after Tyndale's prayer, and following the excommunication of Henry VIII, the king took a remarkable decision and decided that a copy of the **Bible in English** should be placed in every Parish Church.

At the end of Spring 1538 Coverdale began his new edition of Tyndale's translation. On the last page appeared the statement, "The whole Bible finished in 1539", and the grateful editors added, "To the Lord the achievement is due." This edition was presented to the king and as Tyndale's name did not appear in it he approved of it, and this Bible in English went throughout the land. As has already been mentioned, our Authorised Version is some 95 per cent Tyndale's translation.

In the case on the back of Case No 1 is a copy of **"Matthew's" Bible**, 1537. "The Byble which is all the Scripture translated into English by Thomas Matthew . . . set forth with the King's most gracious licence," printed in Antwerp (C37 1 14).

The so-called "Matthew's" Bible was edited by an assistant of Tyndale's, **John Rogers**, working under the pseudonym of Thomas Matthew and paid for by London merchants and printers.

Thomas Cromwell and **Thomas Cranmer** obtained a royal licence in advance for its publication and sale. **John Rogers**, Chaplain to the English Company of Merchant Adventurers in Antwerp, was later the first of the martyrs burnt in 1555 during Queen Mary's persecution of Protestants. The Old Testament was partly Tyndale and partly Coverdale; the New Testament is all Tyndale. This Bible was in effect a posthumously published edition of Tyndale's translation, attributed to "Thomas Matthew", as it was not considered advisable to associate it with the name of Tyndale.

In the middle section of this case is a copy of **The Great Bible**, 1539. "The Byble in Englysche . . . truly translated after the veryte of the Hebrew and Greek texts by the dylygent studye of dyverse excellent learned men . . . Prynted by Richard Grafton and Edward Whitchurch. Cum privilegio ad impremendum solum" — printed in Paris by Francis Regnault and completed by Richard Grafton in London, 1539 (C 18 d 1).

The Great Bible, so called, is a revision by Coverdale of the "Matthew's" Bible, not of his own version of 1535. He also consulted Munster's Hebrew-Latin Bible of 1535 and the Vulgate and Latin translation of Erasmus.

A royal injunction of 5th September 1538 commanded the clergy to set up in every church "one book of the Whole Bible of the largest volume in English". No particular Bible was specified (either Coverdale's or "Matthew's" was then obtainable) but a new Bible was envisaged to be edited by Coverdale and published by Grafton and Whitchurch, with the approval of **Cranmer**, Archbishop of Canterbury, and under Cromwell's control.

Because it could be better and more quickly printed in France, the printing of the **Great Bible** was, in 1538, entrusted to the Paris firm of Regnault which had been printing English service books for over 40 years. Work proceeded under the supervision of Coverdale and Grafton until the Inquisition intervened. The majority of the sheets already printed had been sent to England; the remaining sheets were seized but later recovered. The matter did not rest there; the bold Cromwell sent agents to Paris and got possession of the manuscripts, paper, type and even the printers, all of which were sent to London, where printing continued. The Great Bible was published in November 1539, and a copy placed in every church in the land. Six copies were chained in St Paul's Cathedral in London.

"It is wonderful," wrote the historian Strype, "to see with what joy this Book of God was received, not only among the learneder sort, and those that were known lovers of the Reformation, but generally all England over; among all vulgar and common people; and with what greediness God's Word was read, and what resort to places where the reading of it was. Everybody that could bought the Book, or busily read it or got others to read it for them, if they could not read it themselves, and divers more elderly people learned to read on purpose." Indeed it has been truly remarked that the Word of God itself was the great instrument of the Reformation in England.

Case No 2, third section, contains the **Geneva Bible** (C 17 b 8), printed in Geneva in 1560. The Geneva Bible was the first English Bible to be printed in Roman type and not in the Old English Black Letter type, and with numbered verses.

Large English Bibles were available in the churches, but the people could not take them home. The Geneva Bible was published in a cheap handy quarto edition for private study.

The Geneva Bible and New Testament (1557) were translated and published by William Whittingham and other Protestant refugees from the Marian persecutions, in Geneva, the headquarters of the Reformer **John Calvin. Theodore Beza**, the leading Biblical scholar of his day, did much to establish and elucidate the text.

Whittingham took Tyndale's version as his basic text for the New Testament, and revised it "by the most approved examples and . . . translations in other tongues." Additional words, not found in the Greek but required by English idiom, were for the first time distinguished and printed in italics.

"The Geneva Bible, easily the most accurate translation before the Authorised Version (1611), remained in successive editions the household Bible of English-speaking Protestants for three generations" (The British Museum).

The English Bible, Case No 3 — first section. In this section is the **Bishops' Bible**, 1568, printed in London (C 35 1 14). The return of the Protestant exiles from Geneva, anxious for a more thorough reformation of the Church of England along Calvinist lines, made the controversial comments in the Geneva Bible, and its eventual popularity, a matter of concern to the **Archbishop Parker**. He accordingly instigated yet another version, and in 1566 instructed the contributors — mostly bishops — "to follow the common English translation used in the churches (ie the Great Bible) and not to recede from it but where it varieth manifestly from the original," and "to make no bitter notes upon any text or yet to set down any determination in places of controversy." The different revisers' contributions were to be acknowledged by their initials, "to make them more diligent as answerable for their doings." The work was quickly done and the Bishops' Bible was published in 1568. In 1571 it was ordered that a copy of the Bishops' Bible should be placed in cathedrals and other churches together with a copy of Foxe's Book of Martyrs.

The next item is a Roman Catholic **Rheims-Douai** version of the New Testament, 1582. The Old Testament was not published, because of lack of funds, until 1609-10 in Douai. The translators state that they were very precise and religious in following the Vulgar approved Latin, not only in sense but sometimes in the very words which may seem, to English ears, rudeness or ignorance.

Stephen Gardiner, Bishop of Winchester, had advocated that technical words should be transliterated and explained in notes rather than represented by imperfect equivalents. Many of these words came into the Authorised Version of 1611 and so gained wide and permanent currency.

In 1589 **William Fulke**, Master of Pembroke College, Cambridge, printed the entire New Testament in parallel columns with the Bishops' Bible text, in order to confute what he considered its errors.

In the final section of "The English Bible, Case No 3" is a copy of the **Authorised Version, printed in 1611** by Robert Barker (C 35 1 11).

At the **Hampton Court Conference** convened by **James I** in 1604, a suggestion that was made met with the king's approval: this was that "one uniform translation" of the Bible should be prepared, to remedy the imperfections of current English versions, "by the best learned in both universities." Upwards of fifty scholars were divided into six companies or teams; each took a part of the Bible which they then divided into manageable sections. When a section was complete it was submitted to the other teams for criticism. The final revision was made by a committee of twelve, two members from each team, and the editing was done at Stationer's Hall by **Thomas Bilson, Bishop of Winchester**, and **Miles Smith**.

Rules were drawn up for the translators' guidance. The Bishops' Bible was their basic text. They were also to consult the versions of Tyndale and Coverdale, the "Matthew's" Bible (1537), which contained the work of these two pioneers, the Great Bible (1539) (ie Coverdale's revision of the "Matthew's" Bible which Archbishop Parker had taken for the basis of the Bishops' Bible) and the Geneva Bible of 1560. The **Rheims New Testament**, though not prescribed, was consulted constantly. Proper names were to be in the form already familiar in English. Taking into account rhythm and euphony, the **King James Bible**, better known as the Authorised Version ("appointed to be read in churches"), was printed in a black letter folio by Robert Barker, the king's printer, seen through the press by Bilson and Smith, and published in 1611.

"The Holy Bible conteyning the Old Testament and the New; newly translated out of the original tongues; and with the former translation diligently compared and revised: by his Majesties speciall commandment appointed to be read in churches."

Although the title says "newly translated from the original tongues," the translators aimed "not to make a new translation but to make a good one better, or out of many good ones, one principal good one." They preserved much of the wording of Tyndale and Coverdale; changes were made only in the interests of accuracy and sense. A work of superlative literary quality was thus produced, most unusually by a committee; surely a sign of the operation of the Spirit of God in the undertaking; a book which, in Macauly's words, "if everything else in our language should perish, would alone suffice to show the whole extent of its beauty and power."

In the other side of this case are three examples of Bible illumination. The remaining exhibits in the gallery are of music printing, music manuscripts, children's books and the works of a French playwright.

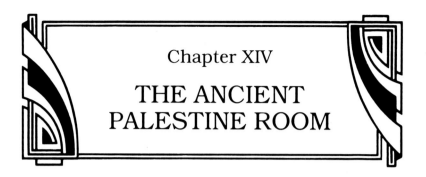

Chapter XIV

THE ANCIENT PALESTINE ROOM

As sometimes a choice piece of a meal is left until the end, so we conclude our visit to the British Museum with a choice tit-bit, the small but very interesting Ancient Palestine Room.

From the Great Russell Street entrance we turn left through the card gallery and then right into the Egyptian Sculpture Gallery. Going right through this gallery and the door at the far end, we find the Ancient Palestine Room on the right.

Once inside, we turn left and proceed in a clockwise direction. On the left-hand rear wall are sculptured portraits of **Canaanites, Amorites** and **Sea Peoples**, from the walls of temples at Thebes. The **Philistines** were among the Sea People.

Plaques Nos 4 and 5 are Canaanites from Askelon, Nos 2 and 9 are Amorites and Nos 6 and 8 are Sea Peoples related to the Philistines (see also Shandara Warriors in Wall Case No 2).

Wall Case No 1 contains pottery from Jordan.

Wall Case No 2 has casts of Philistine heads taken from the temple of Rameses III, west of Thebes.

There are references to certain groups of Sea Peoples in the Amarna Letters.

The first article on the back of Case No 2 is a long sword which was found at Beth-Dagon near Jaffa. Perhaps Goliath's sword which David afterwards used would have been like this.

Next to the sword are the casts from the temple of Rameses III. Item No 1 is a terracotta head, possibly portraying a Philistine from Askelon (No L101). Items No 2 and 7 are examples of **Amarna Letters**. On the evidence of these letters, Col Conder named **Thutmose III** as the Pharaoh of the oppression, thus confirming the date given in 1 Kings 6 v 1. (For study on this matter see Professor John Bimson's book, *Redating the Exodus and Conquest*, obtainable from The Almond Press, PO Box 208, Sheffield, S10 5DW.)

These letters are appeals for help from various commanders in Palestine to the Egyptian Pharaoh — for help in resisting the raiders from the desert, the **Habiru**, now accepted as referring to the Hebrews. The letters were written from **Hazor, Megiddo, Gezer, Shechem** and **Askelon**; they were found by a peasant woman near **Amarna** in Egypt.

This case also contains examples of Philistine pottery.

Wall Case No 3: This case contains jewellery and figurines, some in ivory. Nos 1 to 5 are ivories from Samaria. 1 Kings 22 v 39 mentions the **Ivory Palace of Ahab** in Samaria — this palace had walls lined with ivory. Some of the pieces shown would have been inlaid in furniture. The figurines here are carved in the Phoenician style; Ahab was married to a Phoenician princess, Jezebel (from Samaria, 9th Century BC).

Nos 8 to 10 are ivories from **Lachish**. No 10 has been blackened by fire.

Wall Case No 4: In this case are examples of pottery, including items from **Gezer, Beth-Shemesh, Askelon** and **Hazor**.

Wall Case No 5: In this case are examples of pottery from the period of the Monarchy, 1000–600 BC, from Beth-Shemesh, Gezer and **Jerusalem**.

Wall Case No 6: The items here illustrate writing and commerce. Items No 1 to 4 are jar handles stamped in Hebrew, "Belong to the King" (Nos 132060-61-65-72), from **Lachish**, 8th to 7th Century BC. Item No 5 is a stamped jar handle with the name Jerusalem on it, probably from the time of **Hezekiah**, from Ophel, 5th to 4th Century BC (K1295). Item No 6 is a clay tablet inscribed in cuneiform with an account of tribute sent by the kingdoms of **Ammon, Moab, Judah, Edom** and **Byblos** to the king of Assyria, probably **Sennacherib**.

Wall Case No 7 — Ossuaries and Glass. Item No 1: Such chests, often decorated with chip carving in imitation of woodwork, were used in Jerusalem during the century preceding the fall of Jerusalem in AD 70, to house the bones of the dead after they had been removed from family vaults to make way for others.

Just at the turn of the century a new form of burial had been inaugurated for temple counsellors and officials and rich people, in which the body was entombed in sarcophagi either free-standing or cut in the rock; of such was the tomb of **Joseph of Arimathea**, a rich man and a temple counsellor.

The New Testament tells us that in the garden near Calvary was a tomb belonging to Joseph, a new tomb, a rock-cut tomb wherein never man was laid. The tomb in the garden fulfils all these conditions. Moreover it was evidently never finished, and a hastily cut extension would suggest that the body placed on the bed was taller than the one for whom it was made. The light from the tomb window falls directly onto this bed, and as the original entrance was only 2 feet 8 inches in height, the disciples "stooping down" were able to see the linen cloths lying. Confirmation of this type of burial at this period may be seen in the catacombs at Beth Shearim in the North.

Ossuary No 1 was found in a tomb on the Mount of Olives and bears an inscription in Greek and Hebrew, "Bones of the family NICANOR the Alexandrian who made the gates". This Nicanor, known from Josephus and the Talmud, presented a famous pair of bronze gates to the temple rebuilt by Herod the Great. They were set up on the outside of the Court of Women (No 126395).

Ossuary No 2, with more elaborate decoration, was found in a tomb in the Valley of the Cross, Jerusalem. The lid represents an arcade, possibly part of the colonnade of Herod's temple.

The next exhibit is a reconstruction of a Bronze Age tomb from **Jericho**, 2200–2000 BC. Nearby is a picture of a room in a house of the Mid-Bronze Age, 1800–1700 BC, made by using the articles of that period found in the tomb as patterns. The tomb had been re-used at the later date and re-sealed.

Wall Case No 8 contains daggers, blades, lance heads and spear heads, and daggers of a later date. Item No 12 is a duck bill axe, a weapon with great powers of penetration, and Items No 10 and 11 are socket headed lances, useful for piercing metal helmets. Items No 13–17 are dagger blades and arrow heads of a still later date and of simpler form, 1550–1200 BC. Items No 1, 9 and 12 are from Askelon; Items No 2, 7, 8, 10, 11, 13 and 16 are from the Jerusalem area; Item No 3 is from Galilee; Items No 4, 5, 6 and 15 are from Gezer; Item No 14 is from Ashdod; and Item No 17 is from Tell el-Ajjul.

Wall Case No 9 — THE DEAD SEA SCROLLS: In the spring of 1947 an Arab goatherd, looking for a lost animal, threw a stone into a cave near the ancient ruin of **Qumran**, about half a mile from the north-west corner of the Dead Sea. Hearing a crash of broken pottery, he climbed into the cave and found

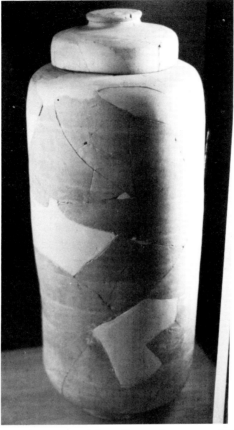

Jar from Dead Sea Caves (see page 180)

Ethnic Types: Hittites   Photograph: BM

jars, such as the one shown here, containing ancient leather scrolls.

In 1947, three complete scrolls, including one of Isaiah, were purchased from Bedouin tribesmen by an antique dealer in Bethlehem. They were brought to the notice of the late Professor Sukenik of the Hebrew University, who purchased them for the Israeli government. A few years later Professor Sukenik's son, the late **Professor Yigael Yadin**, was able to buy four more large manuscripts in America. Following the first discovery, an intensive search of the caves of the area commenced, in which many ancient documents were found, written mostly in Hebrew or Aramaic on leather or papyrus, and one on copper. The copper scroll is now in **Amman**.

Of the eleven caves containing scrolls, those with the richest manuscript collections were Caves No 1, 4 and 11. Cave No 1, in which the jar and cloth exhibited here were found, produced seven large manuscripts, now displayed in the Shrine of the Book in Jerusalem. There were two copies of the Book of Isaiah, one very complete. Normally the Messianic chapter fifty-three is missing from the synagogue readings; the idea seems to be that it was inserted in later years by Christian scholars as it appears to refer directly to the Lord Jesus and His death and resurrection. Professor Sukenik translated the whole of this scroll and on one occasion showed it to the late Rev L T Pearson. The conversation went thus: LTP: "What are we looking at?" PS: "The fifty-second chapter of Isaiah." LTP: "Is the fifty-third there?" PS: "Mr Pearson, it is all there."

As these scrolls are at least 1000 years older than any previously known documents, this was a great triumph for the accuracy of the Massoretic Text on which the Old Testament of our English Bible is based. The cry of the critics was that in all the centuries there must have been mistakes in copying, but the Dead Sea Scrolls are a tribute to the scholarship of the copiers and the extreme care with which the text was copied. Apart from the Isaiah scroll, portions of all the books of the Old Testament were found with the exception of Esther.

Between 1951 and 1956 the ruins of Khirbet Qumran were excavated and found to be the remains of an ancient self-contained community with an assembly hall, and among other features a Scriptorium or Writing Room, in which texts could be copied. An aqueduct brought water from a natural stream in the cliffs.

The most widely held view is that Qumran was a community of a strict Jewish sect called the **Essenes**, who left what they considered to be the corrupted worship of the temple in Jerusalem and retired to the desert to live lives of purity more in accordance with the Law of God.

The copper scroll found in Cave 3 lists the location of a large amount of buried treasure, perhaps that removed from the temple in Jerusalem to hide it from the Romans. This latter would seem unlikely as no one could get in or out of the city during the final siege.

The next item is a notice board giving the history of ancient Palestine from 3100 BC to 640 AD. This text does not agree with the Biblical dating of the Exodus.

Palestine was conquered by **Alexander the Great** in 332 BC. The country was ruled by the **Ptolemies** from Egypt until 198 BC, when it was passed to the **Seleucids**, under whom, in the years following 167 BC, the **Maccabees** and their successors liberated and controlled an area around Judea. This Jewish territory was made a Roman protectorate by **Pompey** in 63 BC, and was finally annexed to the Roman Empire in 6 AD. After the Jewish Revolt of 67 to 70 AD, it became a colony.

Christianity was finally established as the Roman state religion under **Theodosius** in 380 AD, although the process began earlier with the **Emperor Constantine**, after whom Byzantium was named Constantinople when it became the capital of the Roman Empire. This phase ended with the Islamic conquest of 634 to 640 AD, although Constantinople did not fall until 1453.

On the wall opposite are casts of ethnic types, Hittites and North Syrians, taken by **Sir Flinders Petrie** from Egyptian bas-reliefs on the walls of the temples at Thebes. No 1 is of **Hittites**, and Nos 2 and 3 are of **North Syrians**. Such discoveries helped to confirm the Biblical accuracy in recording the Hittites, the existence of whom was very much doubted by the critics.

On the back wall of this bay is a bas-relief showing the Assyrian king **Tiglath-Pileser III** (745–727 BC) standing in his state chariot under a parasol. Above is a fortified city on a mound from which Assyrian soldiers are driving prisoners and booty. The cuneiform inscription identifies the city as Astartu, the Biblical Ashteroth Karnaim in Gilead (Genesis 14 v 5).

This capitulation probably took place in 733–732 BC when Tiglath-Pileser invaded Syria and Israel (2 Kings 15 vv 25–29). At this time **Pekah** was king of Israel and Ashteroth belonged to Damascus.

The last object seen on leaving the Ancient Palestine Room is a large storage jar from Hazor, described in the Bible (Joshua 11) as "the head of all those kingdoms" and which Joshua burnt with fire.

So ends our tour of the British Museum with Bible in hand. It has been a great joy to take you round, and the hope is that on the way a firmer belief in and an assurance of the historicity and accuracy of the Sacred Word has been acquired.

ACKNOWLEDGMENTS AND BIBLIOGRAPHY

Bible quotations are from the King James Authorised Version, 1611.

ALBRIGHT, W F, *The Archaeology of Palestine*, Pelican Books, Harmondsworth, 1949. 582 words, pp 198, 199, 203. Reproduced by permission of Penguin Books Ltd

ANDERSON, SIR ROBERT, *The Bible or the Church*

BARNETT, R D, *Illustrations of Old Testament History*. Quotations by permission of British Museum Publications Ltd

BEZZONI, G B, *Narrative of the Operations and Recent Discoveries in Egypt and Nubia* (John Murray)

BIMSON, JOHN J, *Redating the Exodus and Conquest*, Almond Press, Sheffield

British Museum Guides, British Museum Publications Ltd, 1976. A 1908, B 1904, C 1909, D 1903, E 1906, F 1901

BROMLEY-MOORE, *Foxe's Book of Martyrs*, Cassell, Petter and Galpin

BULLINGER, E W, *The Witness of the Stars*

BURGON, DEAN, *The Revised Version*

CHIERA, EDWARD, *They Wrote on Clay*, University of Chicago Press, Chicago, USA

CAIGER, STEPHEN L, *Bible and Spade*, 1936. Quotation 8 lines p 125. By permission of Oxford University Press

CARRON, T W, *The Christian Testimony Through the Ages*

CLAYTON, P A, *The Rediscovery of Ancient Egypt*, Thames & Hudson

CONDER, C R, *Tent Work in Palestine, The Tell el-Amarna Tablets*

CORNFELD, GAALYAHU, ed. *Pictorial Biblical Encyclopedia*, Hamikra Baolam Publishing House Ltd, Tel-Aviv, Israel, 1964

D'AUBIGNE, MERLE, *The Reformation in England*, Banner of Truth Trust, Edinburgh, 1962. Quotation taken from this work by permission of the publishers

FRANCIS, F, ed. *Treasures of the British Museum*, Thames and Hudson, London, 1971. Quoted by permission of the publishers

GARSTANG, JOHN & J B E, *The Story of Jericho*, Marshall, Morgan & Scott, 1948.

GINSBURG, CHRISTIAN, *Introduction to the Massoretico-Critical Text of the Hebrew Bible*

HABERSHON, ADA R, *The Bible and the British Museum*, Morgan & Scott Ltd, 1909

JAMES, T G H and DAVIES, W M, *Egyptian Sculpture.* Quotations by permission of British Museum Publications Ltd

JORDAN, PAUL, *Egypt the Black Land*, Phaidon, Oxford, 1976

KENYON, FREDERICK, *The Story of the Bible*, John Murray (Publishers) Ltd. Quotation by permission of the publishers

Lion Handbook of the Bible, Lion Publishing plc. Quote from *The Cities of Conquest* by Prof. Alan Millard by permission of the publishers

MARSTON, CHARLES, *The Bible Comes Alive*, Eyre & Spottiswoode, 1938

MEE, ARTHUR, *The Children's Encyclopedia*, c 1914

MEYES, S, *The Great Belzoni*

MORTON, H V, *In the Steps of St Paul*, Rich & Cowan Ltd, London, 1936

PEARSON, LEONARD, *Through the Land of Babylonia*

PERCY, EUSTACE, *John Knox*, James Clark & Co Ltd, 1937. Quoted by permission

PINCHES, *The Old Testament in the Light of Historical Records*

SAYCE, A H, *Monument Facts and Higher Critical Fancies*, Religious Tract Society, 1910. *Assyria: Its Princes, Priests and People*, RTS, London, 1895. *Fresh Light from Ancient Monuments*, London, 1910. *The Hittites*, RTS, 1892

SMITH, WILLIAM, *A Smaller Classical Dictionary*, John Murray, London, 1898

STEELE-SMITH, W E, *The Wonders of the Hebrew Alphabet*

The Companion Bible, Samuel Bagster and Sons Ltd, 1974 edition

TRIGGER, BRUCE, *Nubia under the Pharaohs*, Thames & Hudson, 1976

UNGER, M F, *Archaeology and the Old Testament*, Zondervan, Grand Rapids, USA. Quoted with implied permission of the publishers

VINE, W E, *Expository Dictionary of New Testament Words*

WHISTON, *Works of Josephus*, T Nelson and Sons, 1883

WHITCOMBE & MORRIS, *The Genesis Flood*

WHITE, SYLVIA, *Bone of Contention*

186

WILSON, JOHN A, *Signs and Wonders upon Pharaoh,* University of Chicago Press, USA, 1964. Quoted with the permission of the publishers

WISEMAN, D J, *Peoples of Old Testament Times,* 1936. 7 lines quoted by permission of Oxford University Press

WOOLLEY, LEONARD, *Excavations at Ur,* Ernest Benn Ltd, London, 1963

Young's Analytical Concordance of the Bible, Lutterworth

190

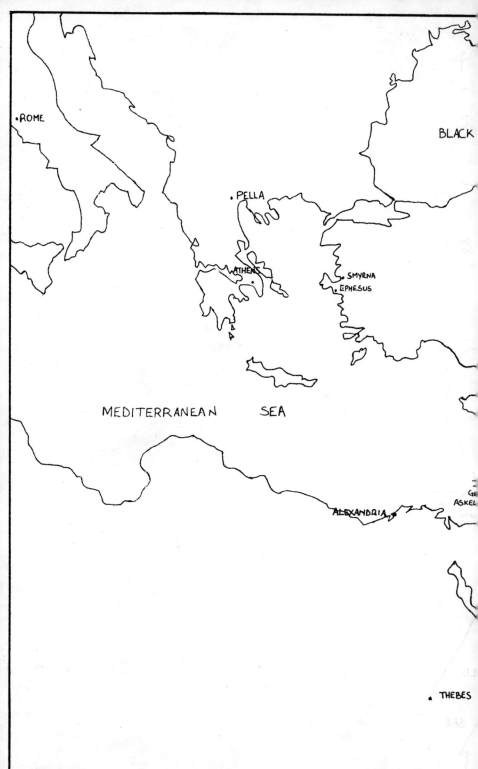

ROME

BLACK

PELLA

ATHENS

SMYRNA
EPHESUS

MEDITERRANEAN   SEA

G
ASKEL

ALEXANDRIA

THEBES

J G Tucker 1986